I0824081

A GIFT FOR

FROM

DATE

PRAYER *in* MOTION

AN INVITATION TO BE FULLY PRESENT,
CONNECT WITH GOD,
AND PRAY WITH YOUR WHOLE SELF

JENNIFER TUCKER

THOMAS NELSON
Since 1798

The exercises in this book are for general wellness and spiritual reflection. They are not a substitute for medical or mental health care. Please consult a professional if you have any health concerns. Stop any activity that causes discomfort or distress. The author and publisher disclaim any liability for outcomes resulting from use of this content.

Prayer in Motion

Published by Thomas Nelson, 501 Nelson Place, Nashville, TN 37214, USA. Thomas Nelson is a registered trademark of HarperCollins Christian Publishing, Inc.

Thomas Nelson titles may be purchased in bulk for educational, business, fundraising, or sales promotional use. For information, please email SpecialMarkets@ThomasNelson.com.

ISBN: 978-1-4002-4802-5 (HC)
ISBN: 978-1-4002-4805-6 (eBook)
ISBN: 978-1-4002-4806-3 (Audiobook)

HarperCollins Publishers, Macken House, 39/40 Mayor Street Upper, Dublin 1, D01 C9W8, Ireland (https://www.harpercollins.com)

Art Direction: Tiffany Forrester
Cover design, cover art, and interior art: Jennifer Tucker
Interior Design: Jeff Jansen

Printed in Malaysia

26 27 28 29 30 PJM 10 9 8 7 6 5 4 3 2 1

For my mom

*You embody all that is
goodness and grace and love.*

*I am deeply blessed
to be your daughter
and so proud to call you
my mama and my friend.*

CONTENTS

MOVEMENT TOOLS

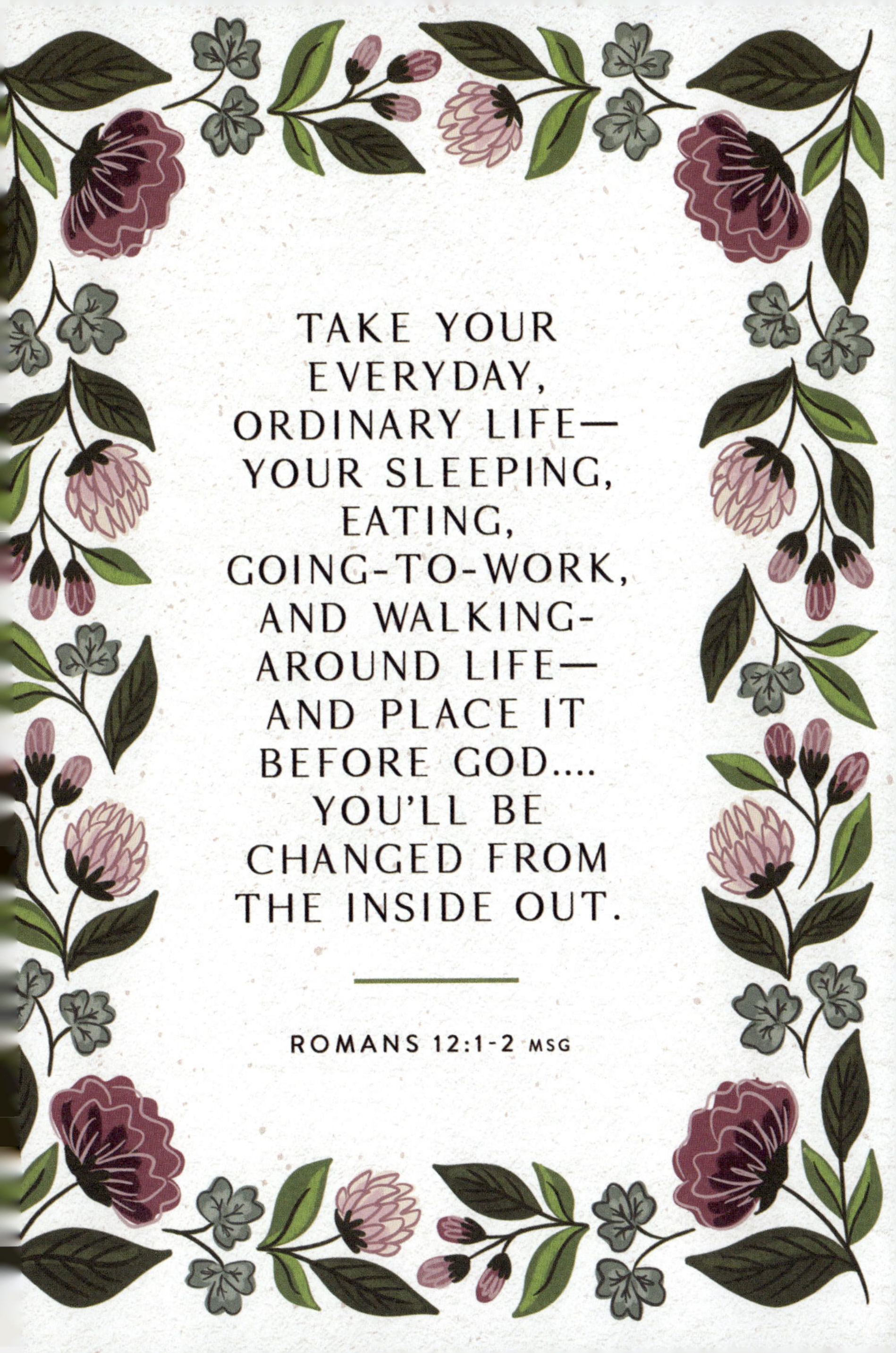
TAKE YOUR
EVERYDAY,
ORDINARY LIFE—
YOUR SLEEPING,
EATING,
GOING-TO-WORK,
AND WALKING-
AROUND LIFE—
AND PLACE IT
BEFORE GOD....
YOU'LL BE
CHANGED FROM
THE INSIDE OUT.
ROMANS 12:1-2 MSG

INTRODUCTION

100 PRAYERS A DAY

The Story of Maewyn

There's an old, old story that has been passed down through the centuries—a legend about a boy named Maewyn,[1] who lived in England long before it was even called England, when it was just an island at the edge of the world. Maewyn grew up in a wealthy family and had a fairly privileged childhood. He spent most of his days playing games and hanging out with his friends, never really having to do any chores or work. His future looked bright and relatively easy.

But when he was sixteen, Maewyn's entire life was completely upended. Pirates raided his hometown, and he was kidnapped and taken to Ireland, where he was sold into slavery. Ireland wasn't exactly a pleasant place at the time—most of the Irish tribes were pagan and godless. Some even sacrificed their children to idols, and many were cannibalistic.[2] A pagan chieftain king named Milchu bought Maewyn and forced him to serve as the family's herdsman. Overnight, Maewyn went from a life of ease and privilege to a life of hard work and cruel mistreatment.

Afraid and alone, he now spent his days in the mountain fields taking care of the king's flocks, and his future looked bleak and lonely.

But instead of spiraling into despair, Maewyn did something that transformed his life: He began to pray. When he looked at the sky, he prayed to the One who "ignites the light of the sun . . . [and] surrounds the stars and tells them to shine."[3] As he felt the grass beneath his feet and the warmth of the sun on his face, he visualized the presence of God shielding him and covering him. He became aware of God's presence all around him—beneath him and above him, beside him and within him. He later wrote:

> When I came to Ireland I spent each day tending sheep and I prayed many times during the day. Thus I grew more and more in the love of God. And as the fear of God increased in me so did my faith, so that in a single day I would pray up to one hundred times and in the course of the night I would pray nearly as many times again. When I was tending the sheep on the mountains and in woods and in the dark before the dawn I would awaken and pray in the snow, in the frost and in the rain . . . for my spirit was always fervent.[4]

Maewyn prayed not just with his mind but with his entire body as he moved through his regular, ordinary, everyday life. As Sandra Pavloff Conner points out, "His prayers grounded him in the earthy and dirty reality of each day and helped him to see God everywhere: in the wind, in the water, in the poor wanderers who traveled by his mountain, and in everyday acts like napping and bathing and stretching."[5] Every part of his life became the source and the substance of his prayers. Every moment, every movement, and every experience became an invitation to pray—to be fully present, to notice God's presence, and to remember His goodness and grace. This practice drew him closer to Christ and brought him a peace that transcended his difficult circumstances.

That boy Maewyn? You probably know him better as Saint Patrick, the patron saint of Ireland. His daily rhythm of prayer strengthened his soul and deepened his connection to God, so much so that many years after escaping slavery, he returned to Ireland as a missionary to the very people who had enslaved him, and he is credited with bringing Christianity to all of Ireland.

Patrick embodied a life of prayer. Prayer was not some stagnant, monotonous task to complete; prayer was the very heartbeat of his life. He lived and breathed in constant communion with God. Prayer moved within him and through him, through every moment and movement of his days.

Christ with me,
Christ before me,
Christ behind me,
Christ in me,
Christ beneath me,
Christ above me,
Christ on my right,
Christ on my left;
Christ when I sit down,
Christ when I lie down,
Christ when I arise.
Christ in the heart of every
man who thinks of me,
Christ in every one who speaks of me,
Christ in every eye that sees me,
Christ in every ear that hears me.

Modern life may feel very far removed from the days of young Maewyn and the iconic life of Saint Patrick. And maybe praying one hundred prayers a day seems a bit extreme and unrealistic. Who has time for that these days? After all, we're not sitting on a mountainside all day with the sky above us and the grass below us. We have kids to get to school, work deadlines to meet, meals to cook, laundry to wash, and the list goes on and on. Most of us do well to remember to say a quick prayer before we eat or before we go to bed, right?

But the truth is, the same God that was with young Maewyn on that mountainside many centuries ago is with you today as you drive to work or shop for groceries or walk down the sidewalk. And you don't have to be a monk living in a remote monastery or a contemplative saint in the middle of a field in order to experience the peace that comes from a meaningful life of prayer. You can pray like Maewyn, right in the middle of your own ordinary life, by simply paying attention to God's presence with you in every moment and movement of your day.

All of life becomes a prayer when we invite God into all our bodily experiences. All of life becomes a continual communion with Christ when we fill our days with rhythms and movements that turn and return our attention to His constant presence and His abiding love.

CONSIDER YOUR RHYTHMS

Rhythms are all around us. Nature has rhythms: The seasons change, the sun rises and sets, the moon waxes and wanes, the tides rise and fall. Our bodies have rhythms of birth and death, heartbeats and breath, waking and sleeping, circulation and digestion. Our daily lives have rhythms—the routines and habits that move us through our days. Some of us may have consistent and intentional rhythms, while others may have more chaotic or reactive rhythms, but we all tend to follow some kind of pattern from day to day.

Take some time to think about your own daily rhythm. Consider the patterns that guide the flow of your typical day. From the moment you wake up until you lie down to sleep, what are the things that fill your everyday life? Is prayer a part of your typical day? How about some kind of movement? What do you do every day that brings you feelings of calm? What causes feelings of stress?

Our rhythms tend to reveal what really matters to us. If someone looked at your daily rhythms (not the ones you wish you had but the actual rhythms of your actual life), what would they say is most important to you? What do your routines reveal about your priorities? What might the current rhythm of your life be revealing about the state of your soul?

Cultivating intentional rhythms and orienting our daily routines around our core values can help anchor our days and keep our hearts tethered to what really matters, no matter what the days may bring. In the following pages, I invite you to consider two particular rhythms in your life: prayer and movement. I deeply believe that, no matter the season or circumstances of your life, by incorporating rhythms of prayer and movement into your days, you can nurture a more deeply embodied way of life that allows you to move through stress, connect with God, and experience greater joy and peace.

CULTIVATING A RHYTHM OF PRAYER

Right here in the middle of our regular, ordinary life is where we meet God. He can always be found in the present moment, here and now—as you groggily roll out of bed, as you pour a cup of coffee, as you drive the kids to school, as you commute to work, as you cook dinner, as you sit on the couch, as you scroll on your phone. He is here. The real question is, are you? Are you fully present in this moment? Are you aware of the presence of God with you right now?

So many of us get caught up in the frantic pace of life, quickly rushing from one task to the next, ruminating over the past or worrying about the future. We rarely slow down long enough to pay attention to the moment right in front of us, let alone notice God's presence with us in every moment.

Prayer is how we can practice this present-moment awareness of God's presence.

Prayer keeps us tethered to God when the storms of life rage or worries weigh us down. When the stress and anxieties of our circumstances press in and overwhelm us, having rhythms of regular prayer can help us remain attached to the safety of God's love and keep us securely anchored to hope.

Cultivating a daily rhythm of prayer is not a new idea. In fact, having a daily prayer rhythm is an ancient practice that can be traced back to long before the days of Saint Patrick. As Tyler Staton explains, "In the Hebrew tradition, which contains the very roots of the Christian faith, there has always been a daily prayer rhythm: pausing to pray three times a day—morning, midday, and evening. In fact, all the great spiritual traditions insist on some kind of a daily prayer rhythm."[6]

Now I know you may be thinking, *Sure, that sounds good in theory, but how in the world can I add more prayer into my day when my life is already filled to the brim, and I'm already overwhelmed and exhausted?*

That's the good news! Creating a rhythm of prayer is not about adding more things to your already overflowing days, and it's not even about saying more words to God. It's about incorporating prayer into what you're *already* doing every day. Prayer isn't a task to check off your Christian to-do list; prayer is about centering your life on the presence of God. I love how Joan Chittister describes it: "Prayer is a way of life that integrates the great values of the faith with the life we breathe. It is not something tacked on to the day. It is the heartbeat of life."[7] And when prayer is the heartbeat of your life, Christ becomes the anchor of your days.

Many of us likely already have some rhythms of prayer in place. We may regularly say grace before we eat a meal, or we may pray with our kids when we tuck them into bed.

Devote yourselves to prayer with an alert mind and a thankful heart.
COLOSSIANS 4:2

Many of us may even set aside quiet time every morning or evening, devoting time to Scripture reading and intentional prayer. These habits are good and wonderful and are certainly beneficial for spiritual growth. Setting aside times for stillness and silence with God, or for meditative prayer practices can be an important part of a daily prayer rhythm. But prayer doesn't end when you say "amen," and God doesn't leave when you close your Bible. As you move through your day and the stress starts to weigh you down, when the to-do list grows and the laundry piles up, when the kids are screaming and dinner is burning, God is still there. The invitation to turn to Him and rest in His love is still yours. Right here. Right now.

What if we could let go of the limited definitions of what we thought prayer is supposed to be and instead embraced prayer as a way of life—as a living and moving and breathing communion with God? Prayer that isn't just spoken but experienced as we walk with Him through the mundane and momentous moments of our days?

ORDINARY, EVERYDAY LITURGIES

Are there any moments in your day that are intentional reminders to turn your heart and mind to God's presence, any rhythms that specifically remind you to pray? Even the most mundane tasks and ordinary chores can become liturgies of prayer that draw you closer to God. In her book, Every Home a Foundation, Phylicia Masonheimer suggests assigning yourself a topic to pray about as you go about your regular everyday movements and tasks, describing this as, "a physical action leading to intimacy with God: liturgy."

Pray for your children as you wash the dishes.
Pray for your spouse as you fold laundry.
Pray for your neighbors as you feed your pets.
Pray for your friends as you prepare dinner.
You can reach out to God as you brush your teeth,
you can talk to Him while you walk the dog,
you can share your worries with Him as you make your bed.

Simply choose a routine task you do every day and make that a time to pray. Start small. Choose just one everyday routine—something you're already doing—and pray as you do that task. Try this for a few days and let that ordinary task become a gentle invitation to turn your heart to God.

MONASTIC RHYTHMS

If you're still not sure how to develop a daily rhythm of prayer, try taking some cues from centuries-old monastic practices that foster rhythmic and repetitive routines that gently guide you to a more contemplative and mindful way of living. I'm sharing three of my favorites that can easily be incorporated into your everyday life.

BENEDICTINE BELLS

Every day in a monastery, bells ring out over the community, calling the monastic heart to prayer. The purpose of the bells is to simply interrupt the busyness of daily life and provide an auditory reminder to pay attention.

What can be a bell in the midst of your day? Maybe it's as simple as an alarm set on your phone, the ringing tone acting as a reminder every day to stop and spend a few moments in contemplation and prayer. Or it can even be something like a wind chime hanging near your window, the call of the breeze that rings through the chimes becoming a call to your heart to pray. A bell can be any kind of sound in your life that stops you and reminds you to pause long enough to pay attention to God's presence with you.

ANTIPHONS

An antiphon is a short phrase based on Scripture, usually from Psalms, that is sung or recited before and after the reading of Scripture during a liturgical service. According to Joan Chittister in her book, *The Monastic Heart*, antiphons "distill the psalm into a single idea that can be pondered and understood."[8] Like a kind of mantra, this short phrase invites you to focus on one singular truth, and to allow that truth to help you reflect more deeply and personally as you contemplate the Scripture passage.

We can take inspiration from this practice by repeating a short phrase from Scripture throughout our day, bracketing our moments in God's Word. Choose something already you do every day—maybe it's drinking a cup of coffee or driving to work or going for a walk—and try beginning and ending that task by repeating a phrase from a passage of Scripture, an antiphon, that will turn your soul toward God. Choose a verse that has meaning for you, words that will remind you of a truth that calms your heart or a promise that steadies your soul. Ponder these words throughout your day, let them become a gentle prayer in your heart.

Here are some examples:

I put my hope in You.
(from Psalm 42:5).

You are my shepherd, and You're all that I need.
(from Psalm 23:1).

I give You my burdens; You will take care of me.
(from Psalm 55:22).

You have been good to me; my soul rests in You.
(from Psalm 116:7).

LAUDS AND VESPERS

Lauds and vespers are structured morning and evening prayer services that mark the beginning and ending of each day for monastics. We, too, can create a similar rhythm by beginning each day with a prayer of praise and ending each day with a prayer of gratitude. Let the rhythm of the sunrise and sunset be a daily call to prayer, an everyday reminder of God's goodness and glory and presence. The embodied prayers I've included throughout this book can be a great place to start. Choose one to pray in the morning as you focus your mind on praising God, and one to pray at night as your turn your heart toward gratitude for God's goodness and grace.

PRAY CONTINUALLY

Cultivating an everyday rhythm of prayer not only anchors our days in Christ's presence, but it also helps us practice 1 Thessalonians 5:16–18: "Rejoice always, pray continually, give thanks in all circumstances; for this is God's will for you in Christ Jesus" (NIV).

Prayer is to your soul what breath is to your body. Just as your physical life and continued growth depend on breathing continually, your spiritual life and continued growth depend on praying continually.

This concept may seem overwhelming at first—after all, how would you have time to do anything else if you're just praying every minute of every day? But continual prayer is not a constant flow of words to God so much as it is a constant orientation of your heart toward God. No matter where you are or what you're doing, you can pray continually when you simply turn and return your awareness to God's presence with you. Ultimately, this practice of intentional awareness of God becomes a continual, open-ended prayer—that is, prayer that never really ends. As you work, as you shop, as you eat, and even as you clean the toilet, the opportunities for prayer never end because God is always with us.

Think of it this way: Imagine you're on a long road trip with someone you love. You may begin the trip talking to each other a lot, but after a while you naturally settle into a comfortable

REJOICE ALWAYS,

pray continually,

GIVE THANKS IN ALL CIRCUMSTANCES.

1 THESSALONIANS 5:16-18 NIV

silence. You may read a book or gaze out the window at the passing scenery. If a song comes on the radio that you both like, you might sing it together. If a thought comes to mind or if you pass something interesting, you may talk about it. You may stop along the way to eat or sleep or put gas in the car. But throughout the entire journey, your conversation is open-ended and ongoing. Sometimes you're talking and sometimes you're silent, but you're always aware of each other and simply enjoying one another's presence. You don't have to reintroduce yourself when you have something to say, and you don't say goodbye to each other along the way because you've never left one another's side.

That's kind of how it is with God. He is always with you. The Holy Spirit is within you and never leaves you. You are never alone. No matter what you're doing or where you are, you live and move and breathe in the continual presence of God. A life of continual prayer is a life lived in this constant, open-ended conversation with God, in continual awareness of His steadfast companionship. Sometimes you're actively speaking, and sometimes you are silent and simply resting in His constant presence as you move through your day. You never have to say goodbye because the line of communication is always open, and you're always ready to hear from Him or speak to Him at any moment.

Cultivating daily rhythms of prayer can help you foster this kind of continual communion with God as you practice shifting the orientation of your heart toward the presence of God in all the ordinary moments of your day as you journey with Him through this life.

This connection with God becomes particularly significant

when life is hard and the way is dark and the road ahead becomes uncertain. When stress and anxiety build, when worry and fear press in, when everything goes sideways and you can't see the next step in front of you, it's this abiding connection with God that keeps you tethered to hope and anchored in peace even in the darkest and hardest circumstances.

He is with you. Even now. Even here.

NO SUCH THING AS A STRESS-FREE LIFE

I wasn't always very good at prayer. Oh, I tried. My young, rule-following, perfectionist heart was determined to do everything I was told would make me a "good Christian." And so I made my lists and I checked off each task: Read my Bible every day. Pray every day. Go to church every time the doors are open. Tell everyone I meet about Jesus. The list went on and on.

But my motivation was perfection, not presence, and so prayer became just another thing to remember to do, another check on the endless list of unrealistic expectations. I didn't pray from a place of love; I prayed from a place of obligation and performance. And when I forgot to pray, I buried myself in guilt and shame, promising myself and God that I'd do better tomorrow.

Meanwhile, I lived with undiagnosed anxiety and depression.

Come to Me...
and I will
give you rest.

MATTHEW 11:28

For nearly forty years of my life, I didn't have words for what was "wrong" with me. I didn't have a real framework for adequately understanding mental health conditions, let alone any way of recognizing the symptoms in my own life. Back then I thought that if I had any kind of mental health struggles, it meant I didn't have enough faith or the right kind of faith, or I didn't pray enough or pray the right way, or I just didn't trust God enough.

So I hid behind a mask of perfectionism, people-pleasing, and overworking. I tried to control every part of my life—and the lives of those around me—in order to avoid the uncomfortable feelings of my then-undiagnosed anxiety and depression. I strove for excellence to a degree that was exhausting. I set self-imposed standards of perfection that were impossible to reach. For so long I ignored the physical symptoms in my body, and I pushed down difficult emotions. The stress and anxiety would build over time until I was on the floor of the bathroom, sobbing uncontrollably. Or the sadness and despair would press in until I shut down and became numb inside.

I shamed myself for how I was feeling, and I lived in a nearly constant state of stress from trying to cover up or flat-out ignore my underlying emotions. It was exhausting. And it didn't work. I couldn't hide from the reality of my struggles forever.

I can still remember the moment my daughter looked at me and said, "Mom, you're *always* sad." She said it as a simple matter-of-fact, as if stating a truth as plainly obvious as "Mom, your eyes are *always* brown."

At the time, I was disconnected from my body in so many

ways. Our family was in the midst of a very long and difficult season of challenges, and I had slowly spiraled into a constant state of anxiety, always bracing for the next crisis. I was going through the motions, doing all the things that needed to be done. I thought I was okay. But my body told a different story. What my children saw was sadness. What my husband got was disconnection, a shell of who I once was. My family got a Jenn who was always tired, often crying, never laughing. And that might be the saddest part of it all—the laughter left. The joy was gone.

I was just surviving, just getting through each day. I felt stuck. I was trapped in a cycle of anxiety and pain, uncertainty and fear. And I didn't know the way out.

I wish I could tell you that I discovered the answer to healing, the miracle pill or magical movement, that turned everything around overnight. But the journey for me has been long (and is still ongoing), and the changes haven't been easy or fast. Over the last few years, relief from the symptoms of depression and anxiety has come from a combination of medication, therapy, prayer, meditation, and movement. I would guess that is likely true for most of us. We are not one-dimensional, compartmentalized beings. We are body and mind and soul, and every part of us is connected to every other part. And so the journey toward healing is woven through multiple layers of interconnected care—by caring for the body, the mind, and the soul.

There is no perfect answer to the struggles and stress of life. The truth is, we live in a fallen world that is burdened with the damaging effects of sin and death. Suffering in some form is a part of all our stories. Jesus Himself even said, "You *will* have suffering in this world" (John 16:33 CSB, emphasis mine). There is no escape from suffering. There is no such thing as a stress-free life. But no matter your current circumstances, you *can* experience the inner strength and abiding peace you long for, even in the midst of deep darkness and difficulty. There is hope. And that hope can begin in a place you may not expect—the place where you carry the stories of your suffering: your body.

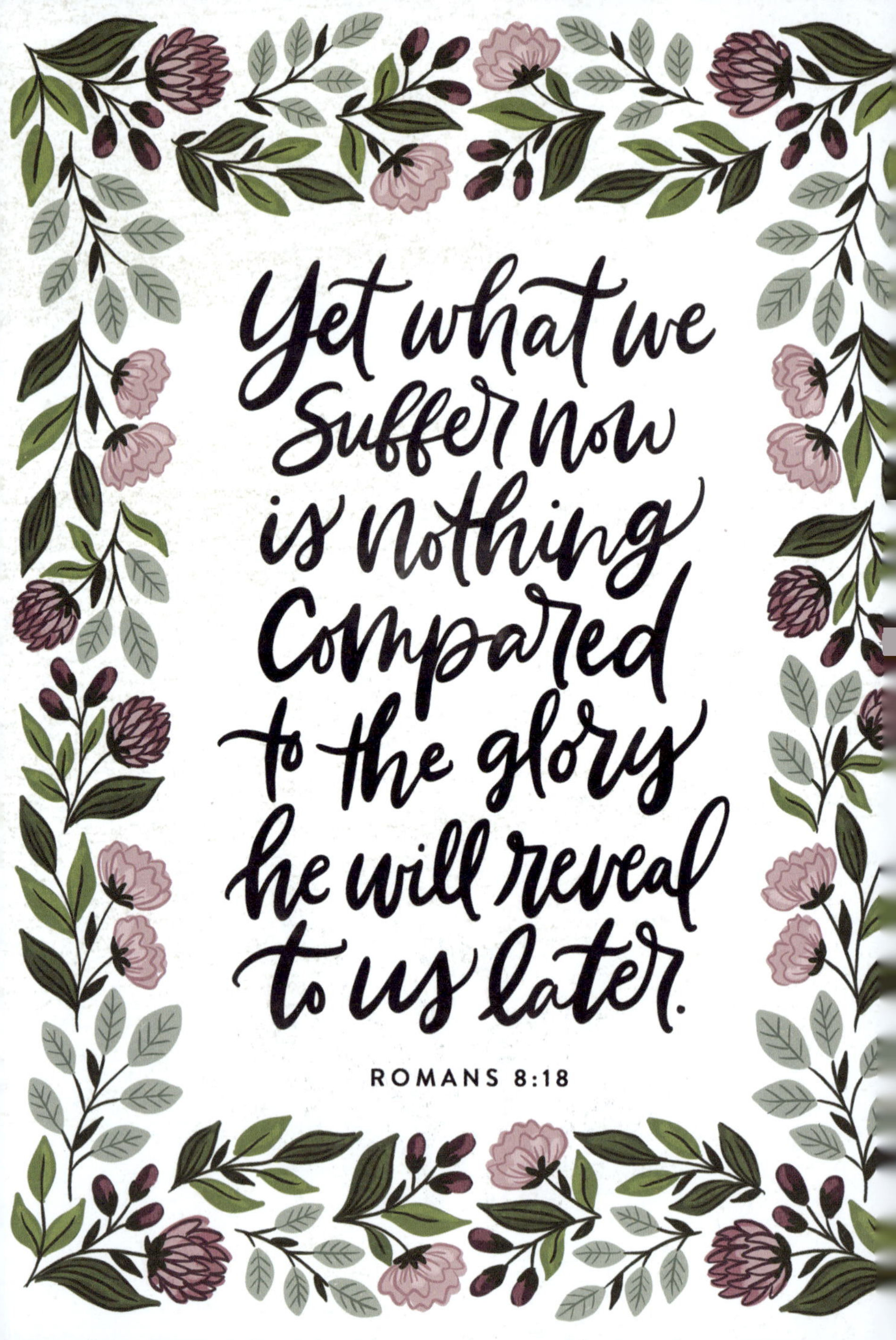
Yet what we suffer now is nothing compared to the glory he will reveal to us later.
ROMANS 8:18

STRESS AND THE BODY

We are designed to feel and to process all our lived experiences through our bodies—through sensations, images, and sounds. Billions of neurons in the nervous system work together to create a communication network between the body and the brain. These neurons are constantly taking in sensory input from our environment and our body and sending messages back and forth to the brain.[9] And these connections affect the way we think, learn, move, and feel. It is all part of the beautifully complex way God designed us to be able to experience life through all our senses.

The ultimate goal of your nervous system is to keep you safe, and it will respond to stress or perceived danger by activating the autonomic nervous system's stress response. A stressful situation triggers a cascade of stress hormones that produces a series of physiological changes in the body.[10] The heart starts pounding faster and breathing quickens. Muscles tense and beads of sweat may appear. This is commonly known as the fight-or-flight response. This means the sympathetic nervous system has been activated, acting like a gas pedal in a car by providing the body with a burst of energy so that it can respond to perceived dangers. Alternately, the parasympathetic nervous system acts like a brake. It promotes the "rest and digest" response that calms the body down after the danger has passed. It is a wise and deeply interconnected system that enables our bodies to be able to react quickly and efficiently in the face of danger.

Dr. Hillary McBride compares the body's stress response to a staircase, with "safety" at the top and "shutting down" at the bottom.[11] When a stressor threatens your safety, she explains, your body is wired to first seek help through social engagement (connection), then to mobilize into action (movement), and finally, if those responses fail, to shut down.

Once you go down a step or two, you can't just think your way back to safety. You must engage your body in some way to reach that state of calm again. Our bodies are where we carry our stress, and it's through our bodies that we can begin to release it. Both movement and connection are integral in helping you move from a place of shutdown to a place of felt safety.

It is completely normal for your body to fluctuate between sympathetic and parasympathetic responses, in and out of activation and deactivation, moving up and down a step or two of the staircase as you move through your day, responding to changing situations and varied levels of stress.[12] This is how your body is designed to self-regulate and maintain homeostasis. And not every kind of stress is severe. Stress is a normal part of life, and in short bursts it can even be beneficial and help increase resilience and motivation.[13]

Dysfunction happens when we get stuck in the activated mode—when that survival fight-or-flight state doesn't naturally ease or is prolonged for some reason. Brittany Piper suggests thinking of it "like a faulty security system, one that's constantly alarming for danger when it's no longer there."[14] Over time, repeated activation of the stress response takes a toll on the body. Research suggests that chronic stress contributes to high blood pressure and causes brain changes that may contribute to anxiety, depression, and addiction.[15] And, as Hillary McBride suggests, "If we stay in survival responses too long and without receiving help, our brains and bodies adapt, making it easier to remain in survival responses than to get out of them."[16]

When you experience difficulty, stress, or trauma, the information from that experience is processed through your body. But if you don't allow those sensory experiences to move through you—if you numb yourself to the painful experiences or disconnect yourself from difficult emotions because you don't want to feel them—your body stores the unfelt emotions and unprocessed information, which you then continue to carry in your body. This can lead to physical and mental health struggles, including chronic illness, increased anxiety and depression symptoms, difficulty sleeping, and even chronic pain.[17]

No matter what caused you to tumble down the stress staircase, and no matter how long you've felt stuck at the bottom, there is hope. You can choose to take steps to move up the staircase toward a place of rest and safety by engaging in movements and connections that help move the stress-related energy out through your body and carry you back to a place of felt safety.

Whether you're carrying deep trauma or you're just overwhelmed with the stresses of life, you don't have to stay stuck on the stress staircase. Our bodies were created to be adaptable and change. Healing is possible.

MOVEMENT AS A CONDUIT TO HOPE AND HEALING

When feelings of stress or anxiety increase and your sympathetic nervous system is activated, your body is primed to move. Stress hormones flow through your body, preparing you to fight or run from danger even if there is no actual danger present. This is why movement can be helpful in calming the body in times of stress. Movement sends sensory messages to the brain that communicate safety, which in turn triggers the parasympathetic nervous system to slow the release of stress hormones and allows your brain to move into a state of calm. Movement also helps discharge any excess mobilized energy that wasn't used so it doesn't become stored in the body.

Be joyful
in hope,
patient in
affliction,
faithful in
prayer.
ROMANS 12:12 NIV

Not only that, but any time you contract your muscles (which is any time you move), your muscles release proteins called myokines, which travel through your bloodstream and affect every system in your body. These proteins can have a significant impact on how you feel and the way you process the stress, from reducing inflammation and regulating blood sugar to strengthening muscles and reducing symptoms of anxiety and depression.[18] One of the first scientific papers about myokines called them "hope molecules" because of the power they have to improve mood and promote emotional well-being.[19] *Myo* means "muscle," and *kine* means "set into motion by."[20] Myokines are set into motion by your muscles every time you engage in any kind of movement. In other words, hope begins to flow when you begin to move.

Movement helps you release stored-up stress and embrace the power of hope. Personally, in my own journey, gentle movement helped me move out of a season of complete exhaustion from long-lingering depression. It seemed a bit counterintuitive. I was so tired and unmotivated. I felt like I had no energy to move at all. But when I started moving anyway, when I began just walking on my little treadmill in my closet, I began to feel alive again. Slowly, slowly, as I moved (and took my medicine and went to therapy), the symptoms began to ease, the fog began to lift, and I started enjoying my life again.

Movement is undoubtedly beneficial to our physical and mental health, but it's important to note that the motivation for movement also matters. When I talk about "movement" here, I am not referring to exercise or workout programs. In our modern Western culture, when we exercise, we are typically doing it to try to lose or maintain weight or muscle mass. We usually have an appearance-based goal in mind, and we are moving our body in ways to reach that goal. The kind of movement I am referring to is not about reaching a physical goal or changing your body in any way. Movement, as opposed to exercise, is focused on embodiment—how you *feel* as you move. While exercise is typically motivated by trying to control or change your body in some way, movement is motivated by experiencing *joy* in your right-now body.

We're not trying to control our bodies; we're learning to listen to them. We're moving to release stress and to experience a bit of calm and joy and hope.

IN HIM WE LIVE
AND MOVE AND HAVE
OUR BEING.

ACTS 17:28 NIV

UNDERSTANDING SOMATIC PRACTICES

Movement and embodiment practices that help release stress fall under the umbrella of somatic psychology. The term *somatics* was coined by professor and theorist Thomas Hanna in 1976, and it has come to represent a field of movement studies and bodywork that focuses on the physical sensations, perceptions, and experiences of the body as a conduit to healing.[21]

Soma is Greek for body. Somatic, or body-based, practices focus on processing emotions or trauma from a body-up approach rather than the brain-down approach that is common in talk therapy. Body-up regulation involves recalibrating the autonomic nervous system, which we can access through breath, movement, and touch.[22] Embodiment practices like somatic movement exercises can help calm an activated nervous system and help us experience a greater sense of calm and peace within our body, not only by getting those hope molecules flowing from our muscles, but also by increasing mindful awareness of the present moment and all that we are feeling and processing as we move. According to psychologist Daniela Ramirez-Duran, research shows promising evidence of the numerous benefits of body-based, somatic therapy and movement practices, including decreased stress, improved sleep, and greater feelings of confidence and hope.[23]

Somatic therapy isn't about erasing traumatic or stressful events or removing difficult emotions. It's about acknowledging the physical manifestations of our difficult emotions and finding healthy ways to navigate them. Grounding techniques, mindful movement, and meaningful connection are all ways we can begin

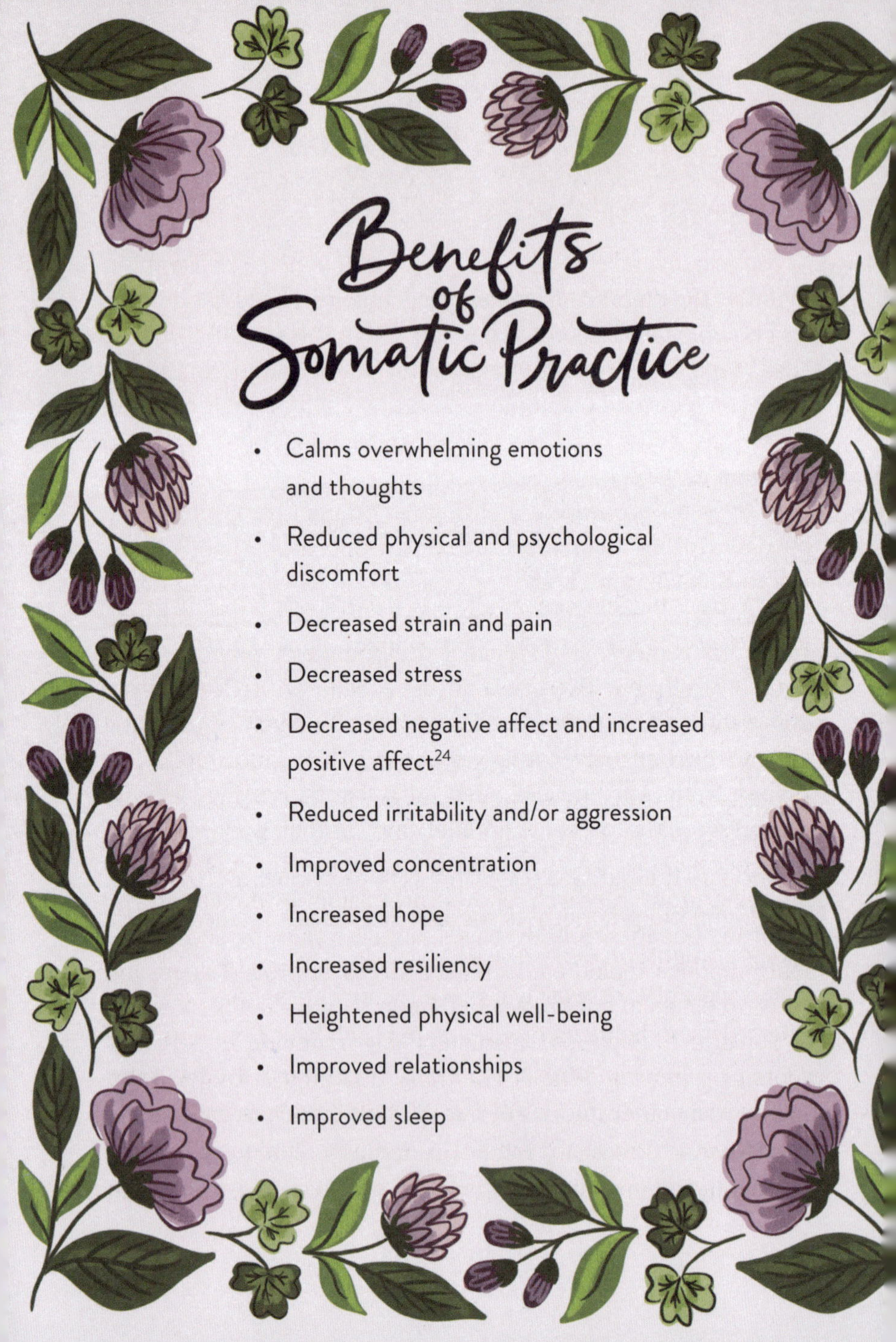

Benefits of Somatic Practice

- Calms overwhelming emotions and thoughts
- Reduced physical and psychological discomfort
- Decreased strain and pain
- Decreased stress
- Decreased negative affect and increased positive affect[24]
- Reduced irritability and/or aggression
- Improved concentration
- Increased hope
- Increased resiliency
- Heightened physical well-being
- Improved relationships
- Improved sleep

to process unfelt emotions and pent-up stress within the body. I've included specific activities for each of these categories in the "Gather Your Tool Kit" section of this book.

Recall that the highest level of the stress-response staircase, and the ultimate goal of your nervous system, is safety. Without a feeling of safety in your body, it is much more challenging to allow yourself to feel and process your emotions. Being able to hold a sense of safety within ourselves, no matter what happens around us, is what enables us to experience a lasting sense of calm and peace in our bodies.

Without safety, all the somatic exercises, grounding practices, and mindful movements simply become another way to perform your healing instead of truly experiencing it.

Safety is experienced through connection. Within the safety of relationship, we find the capacity to move toward embodying our difficult emotions. This is why the deep work of somatic therapy is rooted in a trusting relationship. It is within the safety of relationship and connection that you will find the most beneficial and significant changes.

The activities and exercises in this book only scratch the surface of somatic practices. If you are interested in true somatic therapy, I highly recommend that you start with the help of a trained therapist, especially if you are carrying any past trauma. A therapist can help customize an approach based on your specific experiences, emotions, and symptoms. It may also feel safer to work with a therapist if any unexpected emotions come up in the process.

Although it is ideal and highly recommended to work with

a professional therapist, finding a therapist who is trained in somatic therapy can be difficult, and for many it may not be financially or logistically possible. So I've included a collection of simple exercises and activities that you can do on your own to begin developing a deeper connection with your own body, with God, and with others, as well as tools you can use to cultivate a mindful awareness of your senses and movements that can help decrease stress and anxiety as you move through your day.

Remember, safety is the key. And depending on the stories your body is carrying, cultivating a felt sense of safety in your body can take a lot of time and practice. Be gentle with yourself. Move slowly. Invite God into the process; He's already right there with you. Release your stress, give Him your burdens, receive His peace, and know His love.

EMBODIED PRAYER AS A SPIRITUAL PRACTICE

Somatic exercises and movement alone can definitely benefit your mind and body. But as with anything we do, when we invite Christ into the process through prayer and connect with Him in the small moments and movements of our day, we attach our soul to God and open the doorway of communion with Him. This is where true abiding peace is found: in the presence of the Prince of Peace Himself.

Embodied prayers incorporate gentle body movements as you intentionally turn your heart to God in prayer. These prayers consider the whole self—mind, body, and soul—leading you to

Now may the Lord of peace himself give you peace at all times & in every way.

2 THESSALONIANS 3:16 NIV

notice the sensations in your body while also paying attention to the presence of God with you. Embodied prayers are also a wonderful way to bridge somatic movements with meaningful prayer, helping to decrease the stress you carry in your body while increasing feelings of peace in your soul.

This is not some wild New Age concept. Throughout Scripture, we see prayer as more than just words and thoughts. It is an embodied experience that engages every part of our being. A variety of physical postures and movements of prayer and worship can be found throughout the Bible:

- **KNEELING.** "Come, let us bow down in worship, let us kneel before the LORD our Maker" (Psalm 95:6 NIV). Daniel knelt and prayed three times a day (Daniel 6:10). The wise men fell to their knees and bowed before the infant Jesus (Matthew 2:11). Jesus prayed on His knees the night He was arrested (Luke 22:41).
- **HANDS RAISED.** "Therefore, I want the men in every place to pray, lifting up holy hands" (1 Timothy 2:8 CSB). "So I will bless you as long as I live; at your name, I will lift up my hands" (Psalm 63:4 CSB). "Lift up your hands in the holy place and bless the LORD!" (Psalm 134:2 CSB).
- **CLAPPING.** "Clap your hands, all peoples! Shout to God with loud songs of joy!" (Psalm 47:1 ESV). "This is what the Lord GOD says: Clap your hands, stamp your feet, and cry out over all the evil and detestable practices of the house of Israel" (Ezekiel 6:11 CSB).

- **LAYING ON OF HANDS.** "They had them stand before the apostles, who prayed and laid their hands on them" (Acts 6:6 CSB).
- **DANCING.** "Praise his name with dancing" (Psalm 149:3). "David danced before the LORD with all his might" (2 Samuel 6:14).
- **LYING PROSTRATE ON THE GROUND.** "Then Job arose and tore his robe and shaved his head and fell on the ground and worshiped" (Job 1:20 ESV). "Abram fell face down on the ground" when God spoke to him (Genesis 17:3). Moses lay prostrate before God for forty days and nights, interceding for Israel (Deuteronomy 9:25).

...honor God with your body.
1 CORINTHIANS 6:20

Mindful awareness of God's presence through embodied prayer brings a powerful component to somatic practices. Tapping into the grace and power of the Holy Spirit as you recognize His work within and around you helps bring peace to your mind and balance to your nervous system. Paying prayerful attention to the sensations and emotions in your body, with a focus on compassionate acknowledgment rather than shame or judgment, allows you to name whatever feelings arise and hold them before God, and to let God hold them with you.[25]

What if instead of just pushing through the stressful days, you tried praying through them? What if you could begin to experience every movement of your body as an invitation to pray, every breath and every heartbeat as a reminder of His provision and love, and every sensation as a gentle invitation to be present to all that is right now in this moment?

Maybe you can't raise your arms or move your legs or hear the wind or see the sunset. Even if your body is confined by limitations you never asked for, disabilities you never wanted, or pain you never chose, your prayers are never limited by the boundaries of your circumstances or the limitations of your body.

Your life is your prayer.

Every breath you take is your prayer.

Every prayer is a movement toward Christ.

Every movement, however small, is a hymn of hope.

The rhythm of your life can become a beautiful melody of prayer when you invite God into all the moments and movements of your day.

EMBODIED PRAYER

As you pray this prayer, cross your arms over your chest as if you are hugging yourself, with your palms resting on opposite shoulders.

God of all my days,

I give You every moment and every movement of my day.

May I move at the pace of Your grace, steadied by the rhythm of Your constant love.

Tap your upper arms—left, right, left, right—in a slow, rhythmic pattern as you pray.

(*see "Butterfly Hug" on page 88*)

When I eat,
when I work,
when I walk,
when I sleep,
in every conversation,
in every stressful situation,
in every chore and every task,
in every smile and every laugh,
may Your presence be evident
and Your love be radiant in me and through me.

May the rhythms of my life,
and everything that I do,
bring glory to You.

Amen.

IN EVERYTHING I DO

As you move and pray, turn your heart and mind to the presence of God with you in this moment. Let His Spirit of love and grace move through you.

Prayer is how we connect with God and commune with Him. It is not simply a passive activity, but an embodied experience. We pray with our minds and with our souls, but also pray with our bodies. We pray with our hands and with our mouths, we listen with our ears and our hearts, and we breathe in His love and His life with our lungs. And when we let prayer move through us, and we embody a life of prayer that moves us closer to Christ, we are then moved to use our bodies to live like Christ as we create goodness and beauty, extend love and grace and a warm embrace, fight for justice, speak out for the oppressed, and love all people the way Jesus loves us. This kind of prayer isn't just a way of thinking—it's a way of living. This is prayer in motion.

So whether you eat or drink, or whatever you do, do it all for the glory of God.
1 CORINTHIANS 10:31

GROUNDING TECHNIQUES, MOVEMENT ACTIVITIES, CONNECTION PRACTICES, & EMBODIED PRAYERS

I know the LORD is always with me... my body rests in safety.

PSALM 16:8–9

GATHER YOUR TOOLS

The remainder of this book contains a collection of simple somatic techniques, along with a selection of embodied prayers, that you can use to help reduce stress and increase feelings of safety and peace in your body. These strategies include grounding techniques, movement activities, and connection practices. This is intended to be a "build your own tool kit" resource. You can try the activities you like and keep the ones that are most comfortable for you. Gather the movements and tools that are most helpful so that when you feel anxiety building and you begin to descend the stress staircase, you can reach into your kit and pull out a practical tool to help you regain your sense of calm and take a step back toward rest and safety.

SOME REMINDERS BEFORE YOU BEGIN

ADAPT TO YOUR OWN BODY

Depending on your personal level of mobility, physical limitations, or medical conditions, you can adapt the activities and movements to your own comfort and ability. Focus on the parts of your body you are able to move, on the sensations you are able to experience, and on the creative and unique ways your body serves you.

GO GENTLY

Please approach each practice with care and pay attention to how your body is responding. *Only do movements that feel comfortable and safe to you.*

The activities described here are not in any way a substitute for professional help from a trauma-informed therapist. Trauma is often stored in our bodies—you may not even be fully aware of how your body is holding the hurt of your past—and some movements or awareness practices may uncover difficult emotions that can be distressing or uncomfortable if you have unprocessed trauma. If any activity feels too overwhelming, please stop and seek support.

REFLECT ON YOUR EXPERIENCE

It may be helpful as you try these various activities to take some time to thoughtfully reflect on how you're feeling—both physically and emotionally—before, during, and after the practice. You can write in a journal or simply pray and share with God how you are feeling. Use these questions to help:

- How comfortable was this activity for you?
- Did you feel safe in your body during this activity?
- Do you feel calmness or activation after this activity?
- Were you able to identify any areas of tension? What helped you release that tension?
- As you've tuned in to your body, is there an area that needs care today?
- Are there any worries or areas of stress that you can share with God?
- In what kind of situation might this activity be most helpful to you? Where can you see yourself using this exercise in your daily life?
- What sensations did you feel during this activity?
- What emotions are you feeling right now?
- How can these feelings inform your prayers with God today?
- God sees you and intimately knows how you are feeling today. How does His presence with you and His love for you impact how you will move through your day?

GIVE YOUR ENTIRE ATTENTION
TO WHAT GOD IS DOING
RIGHT NOW,
AND DON'T GET WORKED UP
ABOUT WHAT MAY OR MAY NOT
HAPPEN TOMORROW.

MATTHEW 6:34 MSG

Grounding Tools

Grounding techniques work by bringing your attention to the present moment through sensory input. By engaging your senses and focusing on what you see, hear, touch, smell, or taste, grounding techniques help soothe and settle your body by shifting your focus away from distressing thoughts and bringing your awareness back to the here and now. These simple practices can help regulate your nervous system while promoting a sense of calm to help you manage stress and anxiety.

Grounding techniques are particularly helpful when your thoughts are stuck ruminating on the past or worrying about the future, or when you're faced with a stressful situation and you find yourself so overwhelmed by emotions that they cause you to retreat from the present moment. Grounding can help you stay tethered to the present, and embodied prayers help you stay tethered to God's presence with you. Together, these practices help create a sense of stability and connection between your mind, body, and soul.

BODY SCAN

A body scan is one way you can check in with your body and become more aware of your physical sensations as you intentionally focus on your body and your internal state. This practice helps you slow down and take time to orient your mind, body, and soul to the present moment and connect with how you are feeling mentally, physically, and emotionally. Scanning your body can help you identify how you are feeling and where you are holding any tension.

HOW TO DO A BODY SCAN

- Sit or lie down in a comfortable position and close your eyes. Feel the weight of your body on the chair or on the floor.
- Take a few deep breaths. As you exhale, sense yourself relaxing more deeply.
- Begin the body scan by focusing on your feet.Notice how your feet feel on the floor and the sensations you feel there.
- Slowly, move your attention to your ankles, knees, thighs, and then pelvis. Identify temperature, pressure, tension, and any other sensations as you move up your body.
- When you finish with your lower body, do the same with your upper body. Spend time noticing your torso, back, arms, and hands. include some of your internal organs like your stomach, heart, and lungs.
- Finally, focus on your neck, face, and all the way to the top of your head.

Body Scan

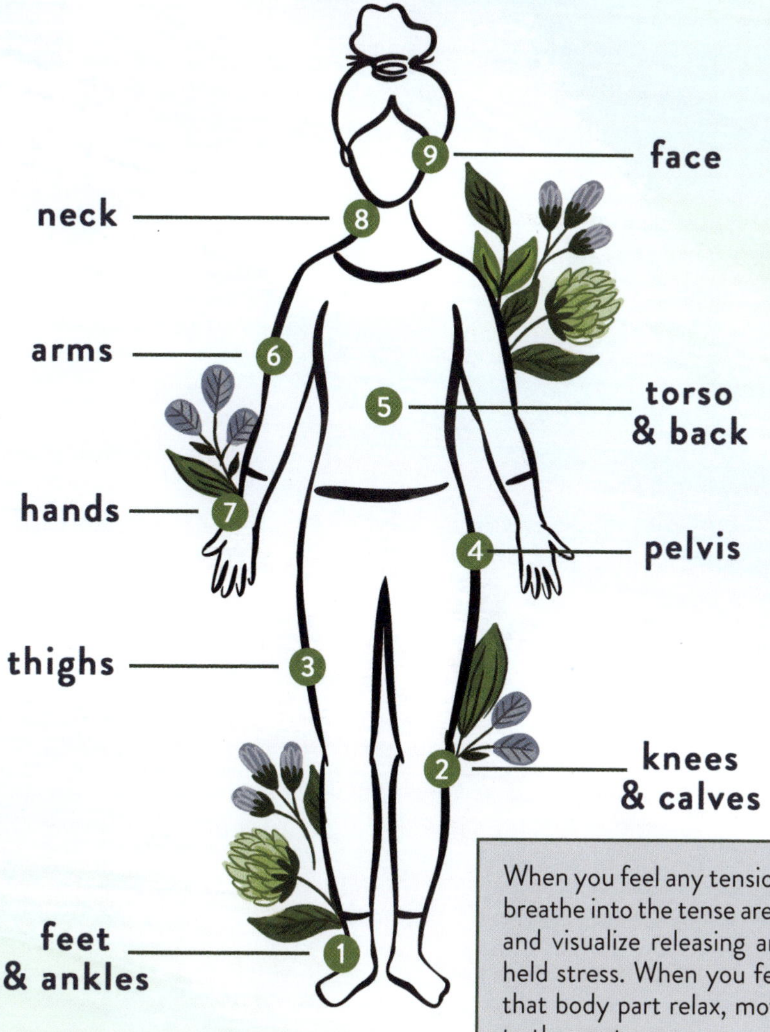

9 face
8 neck
6 arms
5 torso & back
7 hands
4 pelvis
3 thighs
2 knees & calves
1 feet & ankles

When you feel any tension, breathe into the tense areas and visualize releasing any held stress. When you feel that body part relax, move to the next one.

C.A.L.M. BODY SCAN

Psychologist Christopher Willard shared this variation of a body scan, called C.A.L.M., in a post on mindful.org. The C.A.L.M. scan has just four areas of focus: Chest, Arms, Legs, and Mouth.[26] Like a basic body scan, you will focus on each part of the body while noticing any feelings you experience. In this scan, you will also tense that area then release the tension and allow your body to relax.

Begin by sitting or lying down in a comfortable position.

Chest

Bring your attention to your chest and torso region.

Scan your chest as you breathe. Notice the rise and fall with each breath and how your breathing feels in your chest.

- Are you breathing fast or slow?
- Slowly extend your exhale. This can help release anxiety and stress.
- After a few breaths, breathe in deeply and tighten the muscles in your chest. Squeeze everything together. Hold for a count of three as you notice what this tension feels like.
- Relax and feel the tension flow away.
- Resume natural breathing.

Arms

Bring your attention to your arms, from your shoulders down to your fingers.

- Lift and drop your shoulders once and let your arms fall to your sides or in your lap.
- Starting from your fingers, scan each arm, one at a time. Notice how your arms feel. Are they tensed, relaxed, warm, cold, tingly, or numb? Simply notice the sensations while you breathe gently.
- After a few breaths, inhale and tense the muscles in each arm, squeezing your fists, biceps, and shoulders. Hold for three to five seconds.
- Release your arms as you exhale and notice the relaxed, softened feeling in your arms.
- Resume natural breathing.

Legs

Bring your attention to your legs, starting from your hips all the way down to your toes.

- Scan each leg, one at a time. Notice how they feel. Allow your attention to flow through your thighs, calves, and feet.
- Our legs can sometimes shake with anxiety or hold tension and stress. Notice if your legs are communicating anything in this moment. Are they achy, tight, or relaxed? Simply notice the sensations while you breathe gently.
- After a few breaths, inhale and tense the muscles in each leg, scrunching your toes and tensing your calves, hamstrings, and glutes. Hold for three to five seconds.
- Release your legs as you exhale and notice the relaxed feeling in them.
- Resume your natural breathing.

Mouth

Bring your attention to your mouth and jaw.

- Notice how you're holding your mouth. What expression is your mouth communicating? Is it tight, pursed, or soft? Many of us hold tension here and clench our jaw muscles without realizing it.
- Take three deep breaths with long exhales through the nose.
- On your next breath in, clench the muscles around your mouth, face, and jaw. See how small and tight you can make your face. Hold for three to five seconds.
- Relax your face, jaw, and mouth as you breathe gently again. Stretch your jaw open wide and gently massage your jaw muscles downwards.
- Bring your lips gently together into a soft smile.
- Resume natural breathing.

EMBODIED PRAYER

Pray as you slowly scan your body (you can follow the instructions for the "Body Scan" on pages 52–53 or the "C.A.L.M. Body Scan" on pages 54–57)

Heavenly Father,

Thank You for my feet—
with them, I ____________________.

Thank You for my legs—
with them, I ____________________.

Thank You for my belly and my chest—with them, I________________.

Thank God for each part of your body, naming specific ways that body part helps you experience a full life.

Thank You for my back—
with it, I ______________________.

Thank You for my neck—
with it, I ______________________.

Thank You for my face—
with it, I ______________________.

Thank You for every part of my body.

Notice any areas of tension. Tense and release those muscles.

I give You all the places where I carry tension, and all the parts that cause me pain. Fill me with Your peace.

Amen.

GRATEFUL FOR EVERY PART

As you move and pray, pay attention to how you are feeling in your body. Stay calm and curious as you notice any sensations or emotions that arise, and talk to God about what you're feeling.

Consider your body—this miraculous gift that lets you experience all the beauty and sensations of life. So many of us have a negative view of our bodies. We see the flaws, the limitations, the things we wish we could change. But the truth is, your body is a wonder! You were handmade by the hands of God, shaped by the movement of His love, and filled with His divine breath. You only get this one wild and wonderful life in this fearfully made body of yours. Speak kindly to yourself about your body; express gratitude for what your body does for you; be gentle with your pain and patient with your limitations. You don't have to fix or change your body to be enough. You are already enough, just as you are, in your right-now body.

I praise you because I am fearfully and wonderfully made;
your works are wonderful, I know that full well.
PSALM 139:14 NIV

5-4-3-2-1

This is a classic grounding exercise that can be particularly helpful when you are feeling overwhelmed by anxiety or stress. By focusing on what you can see, feel, hear, smell, and taste right now, you anchor yourself to the present moment. This technique helps you shift your focus away from your worries and fears and brings you back to mindful awareness of your surroundings. Take a deep breath and focus on naming:

FIND THE RAINBOW

This is another simple mindfulness exercise that helps you turn your focus toward the present moment. Look around your immediate environment and find something that is:

- Red
- Orange
- Yellow
- Green
- Blue
- Purple

Mindfulness activities like this are also great to do with kids! When emotions are big and overwhelming, it can helpful to help little minds shift focus and pay attention to the present moment—and activities like this one make it fun! You can even make it into a game and take turns naming all the colors you can find.

EMBODIED PRAYER

Sit in a comfortable position and hold your hands together over your heart as you take a few slow, deep breaths.

Heavenly Father,

Teach me to slow down
and to be fully present in this place,
right here, right now.

With your senses, take in your present moment.

LOOK *with your eyes,*

In everything I see,

LISTEN *with your ears,*

in everything I hear,

SMELL *with your nose,*

in everything I smell,

TASTE *with your mouth,*

in everything I taste,

TOUCH *with your hands.*

in everything I feel,
You are here.

Give yourself a hug, placing your hands on opposite shoulders. Envision God's loving presence surrounding you and comforting you as you finish the prayer.

Your presence never leaves me.
Your goodness is always following me.
Your mercy is always surrounding me.

Thank You, Lord, for Your faithful
presence that comforts me,
right here, right now.

Amen.

RIGHT HERE, RIGHT NOW

As you move and pray, turn your attention to the present moment. Let the ruminations of what has been and the worries of what is to come fade as you focus your heart and mind on the presence of God with you right here and now.

Life is always happening in the present. But we are busy and distracted, rushing through our days, jumping from one task to the next with little time to even stop and take a breath. Too often at this relentless pace we end up missing the joy that is available to us where God is always found: right here, right now.

Every moment is an invitation to slow down, to feel, to see, to notice, to pay attention, to invite God into the moment and to rest in His presence with you. An abundance of life is always happening all around you, right here and now—and God is right there with you, in it all. Do you notice Him? Are you paying attention?

You reveal the path of life to me; in your presence is abundant joy; at your right hand are eternal pleasures.
PSALM 16:11 CSB

...in your presence is abundant joy...
COLOSSIANS 4:2

LOOK DOWN, LOOK UP

This is a simple practice of presence that can help open your eyes to what is already around you in the here and now. I first saw Emily P. Freeman share this simple technique on Instagram,[27] and it immediately became one of my favorites for quickly grounding myself in moments of stress. She recommends, "Look up in gratitude and down for grounding at least once a day." It's such a simple thing, but just taking a moment to pause and notice can make quite a difference.

Stop wherever you are.

LOOK DOWN

Notice what's beneath your feet.
Take a few deep breaths and simply pay attention to where you are right now.
Your feet are planted in safety. God is with you right now.

LOOK UP

Notice what's above your head.
Take a few deep breaths and pay close attention to where you are right now.
Your body is covered in love. God is with you right now.

Bonus tip: Do like Emily does and snap a photo of what's below and above you to have a visual reminder of these small moments in your everyday.

GLIMMERS

Glimmers are tiny moments of goodness, joy, or beauty. A glimmer is the opposite of a trigger. Where triggers stimulate traumatic memories or negative emotions, glimmers stimulate positive emotions and feelings of safety and comfort.

Glimmers are not usually big things, but even the smallest glimmers can be powerful tools to help you shift from stress and shutdown to feelings of calm and connection. Noticing glimmers helps ground you in the present moment and activates the parasympathetic nervous system, which can help lower your heart rate, blood pressure, and cortisol levels.[28] Over time, intentionally noticing glimmers trains your brain to seek out safety instead of stress, and to see moments of goodness instead of mountains of problems.

Glimmers are gifts from our good and loving God. Our lives are surrounded by goodness and grace, if we only open our eyes to see it.

Not sure how to identify a glimmer? Consider these questions:

- What brings you moments of delight?
- What brings you feelings of hope?
- What makes you feel safe or comfortable?
- What gives you joy?
- What makes you smile?

GO ON A GLIMMER HUNT AND WRITE DOWN FIVE GLIMMERS YOU FIND

For each glimmer you find, take your time to do the following:

PAUSE AND NOTICE.
Slow down and really pay attention to the tiny gift of goodness.

FEEL IT FULLY.
Recognize how you feel when you notice the glimmer, and be fully present to that feeling in the moment.

GIVE THANKS.
Express gratitude to God for the glimmers that surround you.

EMBODIED PRAYER

Creator of heaven and earth,

Focus on the sensory input your body is receiving as you pray. Pay attention to what you see, touch, hear, smell, and even taste.

I praise You for the gift of
my senses, through which
I get to experience the
glimmers of Your goodness
all around me.

I pause and consider what I see:
(Name what you see right now.)

Pause to consider the things you name.

I pause and consider what I can touch:
(Name something you can touch right now.)

What glimmers of God's goodness do you find as you pay attention to your senses?

I pause and consider what I hear:
(Name something you hear right now.)

I pause and consider what I smell:
(Name something you smell right now.)

I pause and consider what I taste:
(Name something you can taste right now.)

As I mindfully walk through my day, may I take time to pause and consider the wildflowers and the birds, the sounds and the textures in my life. Help me to keep noticing the glimmers of Your goodness all around me.

Amen.

TASTE AND SEE

As you move and pray, turn your attention to the goodness that surrounds you.

Life is meant to be a sensory experience. All of creation is filled with countless sights, sounds, smells, tastes and textures. The sunsets that paint the horizon with color, the of sound of waves crashing on the shore, the sweet and juicy fruit that grows from trees, the scent of roses in full bloom, the feeling of grass under your feet and the wind in your hair—all of life is a sensory buffet intended to help us "taste and see that the Lord is good" (Psalm 34:8). Our senses are a gift from our loving Creator, the One who speaks His love over us and through us every moment of every day. But we don't always notice, we don't always pay attention. Experience this present moment through all of your senses, and notice the goodness of God in the often-overlooked sights, sounds, smells, and textures that are all around you.

Open your mouth and taste, open your eyes and see—how good God is.

PSALM 34:8 MSG

LET US
HOLD TIGHTLY
WITHOUT
WAVERING
TO THE HOPE
WE AFFIRM,
FOR GOD CAN
BE TRUSTED
TO KEEP HIS
PROMISE.

1 CORINTHIANS 6:20

ANCHOR OBJECT

An anchor object can be helpful any time you need something tangible to ground you in the present moment. Find and keep a small item that you find interesting to look at or hold. Choose something that can easily be tucked into your pocket or purse. Examples can be a rock, a piece of jewelry, or a ribbon—anything that can fit in your hand. If you don't have an item handy, you can choose an object from your surroundings to focus on instead.

Hold the item in your hand. Notice its texture, shape, and colors. Notice its weight and temperature. This simple act of focusing on one small thing in the present moment can help calm anxious thoughts and gently bring your awareness back to the here and now.

I have a small wooden cross that I like to hold as I read my Bible or pray. Holding something in my hands helps ground me in the moment, and it also reminds me of God's presence. I have one in my purse that I can easily grab when I'm away from home and feeling stressed. I usually say a simple prayer when I hold it, redirecting my thoughts to the One who calms my soul.

ANCHOR PRAYER

Also called a breath prayer, an anchor prayer is a very short prayer based on Scripture that is spoken to the rhythm of your breathing. The breath is commonly used as an anchor during mindfulness and grounding practices because your breath is always available to you, and deep, slow breaths have an incredible ability to help regulate your nervous system, sending signals directly to your brain that you are safe. Connecting prayer to the breath allows you to calm the physical symptoms of anxiety while connecting your mind and soul to Christ in prayer.

Simply focus on your breath as you breathe normally. Thank God for each breath, then repeat a short prayer in your mind as you slowly inhale and exhale.

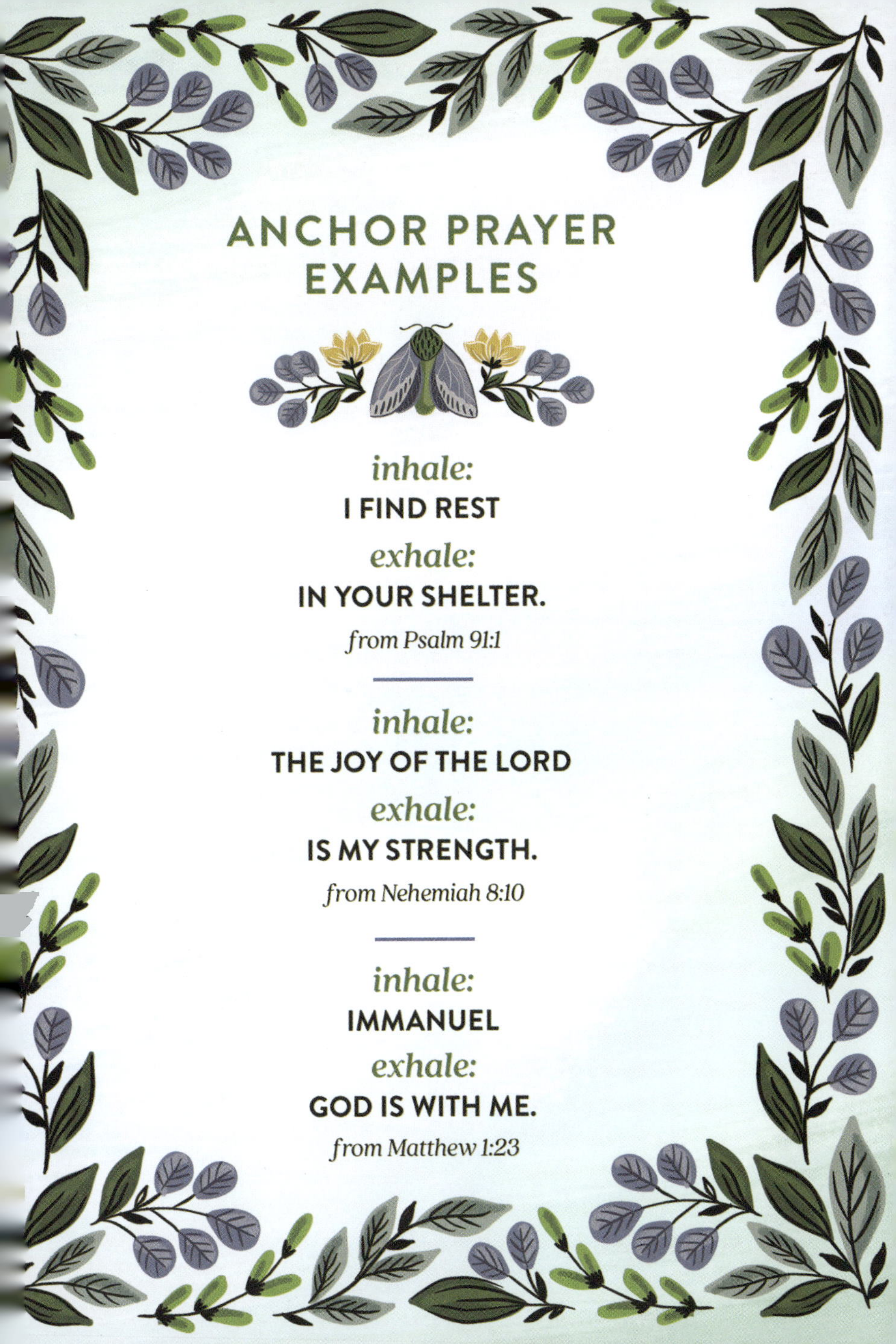

ANCHOR PRAYER EXAMPLES

inhale:

I FIND REST

exhale:

IN YOUR SHELTER.

from Psalm 91:1

---

inhale:

THE JOY OF THE LORD

exhale:

IS MY STRENGTH.

from Nehemiah 8:10

---

inhale:

IMMANUEL

exhale:

GOD IS WITH ME.

from Matthew 1:23

EMBODIED PRAYER

Sit or stand for this prayer—whatever position is most comfortable.

God of the wind and waves,

You already know how worries tend to fill my mind

Join your hands over your chest and sway gently from side to side as you tell God about your worries and fears.

You know how fear grips my heart when I think about ________
(Name a worry or fear that has you feeling unsteady or tossed about on the waves.)

Examples:
The child who is struggling
The future that is unknown
The pain that presses in
The job that is uncertain
The changes that are hard
The world that is in chaos

Continue to gently sway as you stretch your arms out, palms up.

In the midst of the wind and the waves, You are the anchor that holds me steady.

Guide me safely beneath the shelter of Your loving presence, where I find rest in the shadow of Your wings.

Amen.

THE ANCHOR

As you move and pray, turn your attention and awareness to the deep and abiding love of God. God loves you infinitely and completely. His love is unrelenting and unending, faithful and enduring. His love is not based on your abilities, your health, or your strength. There's nothing you can do to earn His love. He already loves you. Period.

Sometimes we forget how loved we really are. Fear and doubt and pain can feel more powerful than His love as worries and anxieties cloud our minds. But when we create rhythms that continuously turn our hearts to Christ and remind us of His love, we can endure any storm that may come.

Prayer is the anchor that keeps you tethered to Christ. An abiding communion with God is what can help you hold tight to hope and stay rooted in peace, even when the waves of worry crash down on you or fear threatens to uproot you. Turn to Christ. Rest in the shadow of His love. You are safe and held and loved.

Whoever dwells in the shelter of the Most High
will rest in the shadow of the Almighty.
PSALM 91:1 NIV

BREATHWORK

Breathwork is a term that refers to a variety of breathing techniques that involve conscious control of breathing patterns. Intentional deep breathing exercises have been shown to reduce blood pressure and heart rate, improve mood, and reduce symptoms of anxiety.[29] Breathing gives you a direct connection to your nervous system, and changing your breathing patterns can directly affect the signals being sent from your nervous system to your brain. Slow, deep breaths send signals of safety and can help ease the symptoms of stress.

There are many different breathing techniques, and I've only included a small sample here. Give them a try and see which ones are most calming for you. Try starting your day with a few intentional deep breaths, or pause throughout your day when you feel stress building and purposefully slow your breathing. Try focusing your attention on your breath and on the present moment. It's normal for tasks and to-dos to come to mind as you begin to breathe. Be gentle with your mind doing its job (thinking), and compassionately return your focus to your breath.

Bonus tip: You can easily incorporate an anchor prayer or antiphon (a phrase from Scripture) as you breathe to focus your thoughts on the truth in God's Word.

Note: *If you have any underlying health conditions, such as asthma or COPD, consult with your healthcare provider before practicing deep-breathing techniques to make sure they are safe for your body.*

BOX BREATHING

Also known as square breathing, this diaphragmatic breathing exercise is a relaxation technique that can help calm the physical symptoms of anxiety and stress.

- **Inhale:** Breathe in slowly through your nose for a count of four.
- **Hold:** Hold your breath for a count of four.
- **Exhale:** Breathe out slowly through your mouth for a count of four.
- **Hold:** Hold your breath again for a count of four.
- Repeat the cycle for as long as desired.

BUTTERFLY BREATHING

I first saw this technique on *Sesame Street*, and it's a great one for kids and adults alike![30] Simply raise and lower your arms (like a butterfly) as you slowly inhale and exhale to help calm big emotions and promote feelings of safety in your body.

- **Start:** Stand or sit with your arms at your sides.
- **Inhale:** As you take a deep breath in, slowly raise your arms out to your sides and above your head.
- **Exhale:** As you breathe out slowly through your mouth, lower your arms back to your sides.

I bless you every time I take a breath . . .

PSALM 63:3 MSG

PHYSIOLOGICAL SIGH

This deep-breathing technique is characterized by a double inhalation, followed by a single, longer exhalation. The longer exhalation activates the parasympathetic nervous system, which slows the heart rate and has an overall soothing effect on the body.[31]

- **Inhale** through nose once. Pause.
- **Inhale** through nose again.
- **Exhale** through mouth for six to eight seconds.
- Repeat two to three times.

BUMBLEBEE BREATH (HUM!)

Humming stimulates the vagus nerve, the emotionally sensitive nerve that is located in the brainstem and travels down through the neck, thorax, and abdomen. The vagus nerve is directly connected to your nervous system and sends sensory signals from your body to your brain. Stimulating this nerve through an activity like humming can help calm the parasympathetic nervous system and help you feel safe in your body.

- Sit up straight in a comfortable position and inhale through your nose.
- As you exhale, push your breath out with a soft hum.
- Feel the vibrations in your chest, throat, and face. Imagine that the humming sound sends vibrations all along the path of the vagus nerve.
- Repeat three times, or as many times as feels soothing and comfortable to you.

EMBODIED PRAYER

Sit in a comfortable position and slow your breathing. Inhale deeply and exhale slowly as you pray this prayer.

Lord,

in Your presence,
I will simply breathe.

I inhale and I exhale.
Every breath is a gift of Your grace.

I breathe in Your love;
I breathe out my worries.

I breathe in Your grace;
I breathe out my fear.

As I breathe, I give You thanks.
You give me breath and life in every moment and movement,
and You will give me everything I need.

Amen.

BREATHING GRACE

As you move and pray, turn your attention to your breath. Breathe deeply and slowly and notice how your body begins to calm as you intentionally slow your breathing.

The breath of God is the source of all life. In the very beginning He breathed the world into existence, and His breath gave life into mankind. And even now, it's His breath that moves in and out of our lungs and gives life to every one of our organs and cells. If God can birth stars and galaxies with a word and give life and breath to everything on this beautiful planet, is there anything He can't do? Is there any need that He can't meet?

Breathe in right now and be reminded of the gift of life God has given you. Inhale His love and goodness deep into your soul. Now exhale all your worries and fears. Breathe out whatever is weighing you down and let the breath of God fill you with renewed peace as you trust Him to meet all of your needs.

He himself gives life and breath
to everything, and he satisfies every need.
ACTS 17:25

SELF-SOOTHING TECHNIQUES

When the world is overwhelming or your worries are weighing you down, it can be tempting to want to run toward distraction and disconnection to avoid the uncomfortable feelings of anxiety that fill your body. But anxiety tends to persist or even get worse when we ignore it, and this can lead to increased feelings of tension, fatigue, and numbness over time.

Instead of ignoring or avoiding uncomfortable emotions or anxious thoughts, it can often be much more helpful to pay attention to these feelings with curiosity and self-compassion. You can then engage your body through self-soothing techniques to help regulate your nervous system and increase feelings of safety and comfort.

The following four exercises focus on using gentle, intentional touch as a way to self-soothe, but there are many different kinds of self-soothing techniques involving the breath, sensation, movement, or touch. In fact, most of the practices in this tool kit are intended to be self-soothing tools that you can use at any time to help calm your nervous system in times of stress.

BUTTERFLY HUG
CONTAINMENT HUG
Self-Soothing
TECHNIQUES
SELF-HOLDING
PAT YOURSELF DOWN

CONTAINMENT HUG

The containment hug, or self-holding, is a technique created by Dr. Peter Levine, creator of Somatic Experiencing,[32] to calm the nervous system and connect the body to a sense of safety. Physical touch can be a powerful tool for healing. A study has found that oxytocin—a hormone released by touch and known to play a major role in feelings of attachment and love—is also released through self-hugs, suggesting they could offer the same benefits as other forms of touch.[33]

When you're anxious or overwhelmed, try using the Containment Hug:

- Sit down and wrap your arms around yourself. Cross your right arm over your chest, placing your hand near your heart. Then cross your left arm over your right, placing your hand on your right shoulder.
- Focus on what it feels like to be hugged and held. Envision the everlasting arms of God holding you right now in this moment. This can make you feel contained, which can help you feel safe.
- Notice the container you're creating around yourself with your emotions and feelings. Allow your feelings to simply exist, without judgment, until you feel calm and safe.

SELF-HOLDING

Focus on bringing your awareness to the present moment and the sensations you feel. You can pray as you do this exercise, turning your thoughts away from whatever may be worrying you and giving it all to God, knowing He is holding you and you are safe.

- Place one hand on your heart and the other on your belly.
- Close your eyes and take slow, deep breaths.
- Apply gentle pressure with your hands.
- Focus your attention on the warmth and support of your touch. You can also pray a small anchor prayer to turn your heart toward God, reminding your soul that you are safe and held and loved.
- Continue as long as needed.

BUTTERFLY HUG

The butterfly hug is another kind of self-hug that incorporates a gentle tapping on your arms as you hold yourself.

- Cross your arms over your chest as if you are hugging yourself, with your right palm resting on your left shoulder and your left palm resting on your right shoulder.
- Maintain gentle, steady breathing. Try inhaling through your nose and exhaling through your mouth.
- If it feels safe for you, close your eyes. If you would like to have your eyes open, just lower them to a point in front of you and soften your gaze.
- Begin to tap your upper arms: left, right, left, right in a slow, rhythmic pattern.
- Continue tapping for one to three minutes, or as long as feels best for you.

PAT YOURSELF DOWN

Patting yourself down brings conscious awareness to your body and the experience of sensations, rather than being stuck in your head. Sudden stimulation of nerves through this kind of touch disrupts anxious thought patterns, and the firm sensation of touch increases blood flow and stimulates the parasympathetic nervous system.

How to pat yourself down:

- Slightly cup your hands like you're trying to hold water in each hand.
- Beginning at the top of your head, gently pat your cupped hand slowly and repetitively against your body, alternating between left and right hands.
- Pat your whole body down: from your head, shoulders, chest, belly, thighs, and knees all the way down to your feet.

EMBODIED PRAYER

Heavenly Father,

Lie down in a comfortable position.	As I lie down in stillness, I know You are with me. Right here, right now.
Pause and consider God's presence.	As I relax my muscles, let rest flow through my body:
Scan your body, intentionally relaxing each muscle as you consider before God how you are feeling, both physically and emotionally.	I rest my legs. *(pause)* I rest my arms. *(pause)* I rest my torso. *(pause)* I rest my head. *(pause)* Your everlasting arms are beneath me, holding me up and holding me together.
Name a specific place where you are holding pain or tension.	I carry the weight of so many worries. I feel the burden right now in my ____________________.
Open your hands. Tell God your worries as you lift your open hands up in the air.	I open my hands and my heart. I release these worries to You, and I receive Your grace.
Move your open hands and rest them on your chest, over your heart.	Fill my heart with joy, knowing that no matter what happens, Your everlasting arms are always underneath me. Right here, right now, and forever and ever.

Amen.

HELD IN HIS ARMS

As you move and pray, turn your heart and mind to the presence of God with you in this moment. Remind your soul that you are not alone. God is with you.

Notice the places where your body is carrying pain or tension. Pay attention to how you feel both physically and emotionally as you listen to the story your body is holding and become aware of the burdens you may be carrying.

Imagine your whole body, pain and tension and burdens and all, tucked into the gentle hands of God. He is holding you right now. He is riding through the heavens, right to you—to help you and to hold you. No matter what happens today or tomorrow or in any of the moments to come, underneath it all you will always find His everlasting arms.

There is no one like the God of Israel. He rides across the heavens to help you, across the skies in majestic splendor. The eternal God is your refuge, and his everlasting arms are under you.

DEUTERONOMY 33:26–27 NLT

PRACTICE GRATITUDE

Gratitude is a powerful tool for your tool kit. Studies have shown that gratitude helps decrease symptoms of depression and anxiety, supports heart health, and improves sleep. Gratitude positively affects the vagus nerve, causing physiological changes in your body that activate the parasympathetic nervous system, lowering your blood pressure and calming your body.[34]

What are you thankful for right now in this moment? Try making it a daily habit to name at least three things you're grateful for every day. Here are some prompts to help you get started:

- Something that made you smile or laugh
- A happy memory
- Someone who showed you kindness
- Something you learned
- Something you saw, something you heard, or something you touched
- Something in nature
- A pet, a friend, or a coworker
- A food or drink you enjoy
- A simple delight
- An activity you enjoy
- Something that makes you feel calm
- A smell, a taste, or a texture you like
- Someone you love
- A place where you feel safe
- A song you love or a book you've read

Let petitions and praises shape your worries into prayer
PHILIPPIANS 4:6 MSG

FOREST BATHING

A simple way to practice grounding is to go outside and spend time in nature! Pay attention to creation. God has filled our world with a million things to see and experience in the present moment, and neuroscience research has shown that our brains respond in amazing ways to nature. From a stroll through a city park to a day spent hiking in the wilderness, exposure to nature has been linked to many benefits, including improved attention, decreased stress levels, better mood, reduced risk of psychiatric disorders, and even an increase in empathy and cooperation.[35] It also improves cognitive function, brain activity, blood pressure, and sleep.[36] Research shows that just twenty minutes of contact with nature lowers stress hormones,[37] helping our nervous system move into the parasympathetic state of rest and restoration.

The Japanese call this intentional, mindful time in nature "forest bathing,"[38] and it is simply about being in nature and connecting with it through our senses. Ann Voskamp refers to it as "Glory Soaking," stating that "God sings close over us with spread of sky, God stuns and awes with painted sunrises, God unravels stress with His choreographic dance of stars, God enfolds us everywhere in surround sound: '*Glory, glory, glory, I am glory and I fill everything with glory so why fill with worry?*'"[39]

We live in a world of fireflies and waterfalls, rainbows and

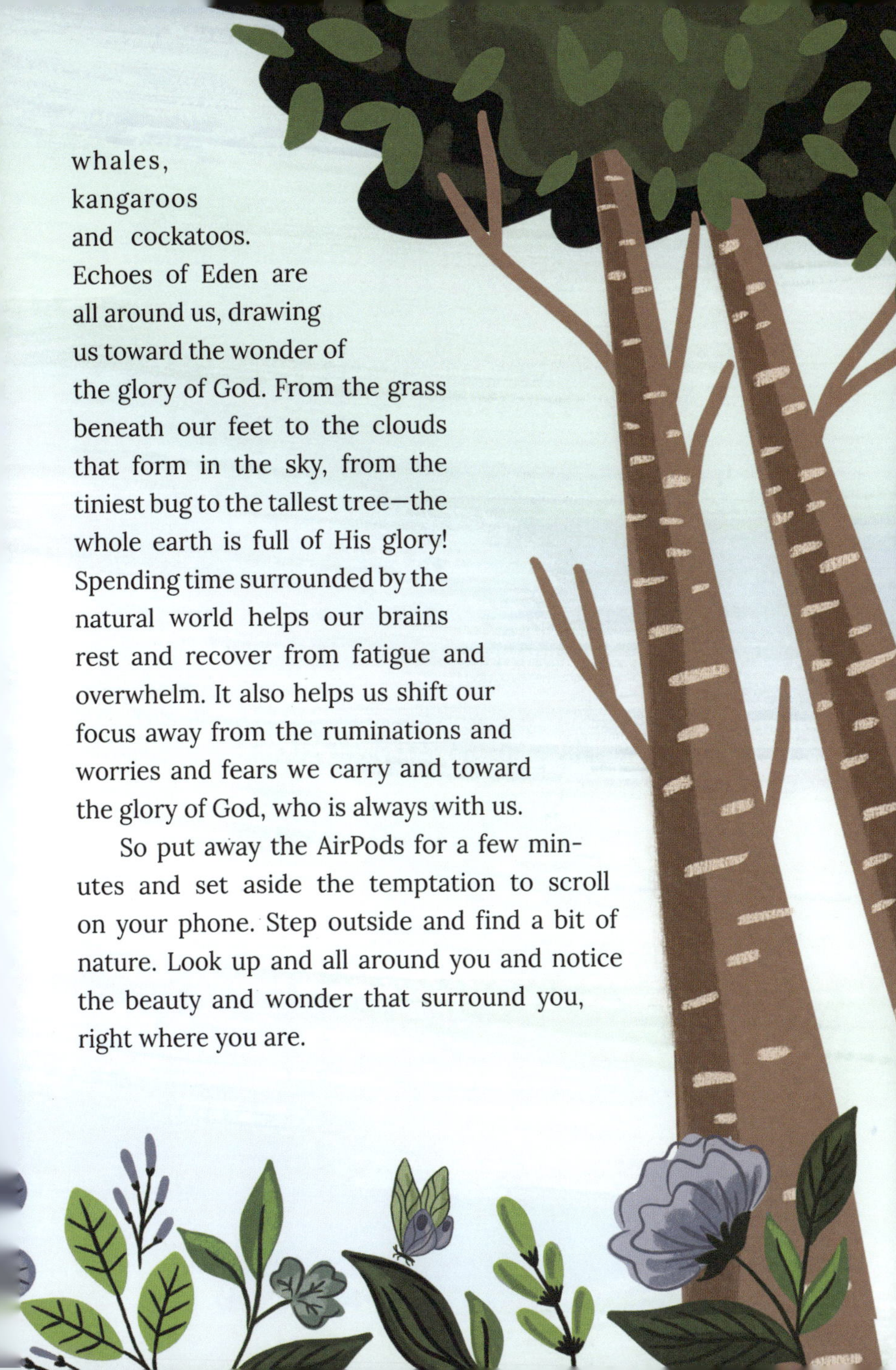

whales,
kangaroos
and cockatoos.
Echoes of Eden are all around us, drawing us toward the wonder of the glory of God. From the grass beneath our feet to the clouds that form in the sky, from the tiniest bug to the tallest tree—the whole earth is full of His glory! Spending time surrounded by the natural world helps our brains rest and recover from fatigue and overwhelm. It also helps us shift our focus away from the ruminations and worries and fears we carry and toward the glory of God, who is always with us.

So put away the AirPods for a few minutes and set aside the temptation to scroll on your phone. Step outside and find a bit of nature. Look up and all around you and notice the beauty and wonder that surround you, right where you are.

Notice and observe what your senses show you:

WHAT DO YOU SEE?

What colors and shapes do you see in the sky and clouds?
Do you see flowers or tree branches?

WHAT DO YOU FEEL?

Can you feel the breeze on your skin?
Can you touch the bark of a tree, the petals of a flower, or the grass beneath your feet?

WHAT DO YOU HEAR?

Can you hear the wind blowing?
Can you hear any animals or birds?
Can you hear the hum of the insects?

Focus on the present moment, and know that God is with you. His glory surrounds you as you are surrounded by His creation.

> If access to nature is not easy for you, whether because of your location or mobility challenges, you can even just look out an open window and gaze at the sky. Watch the clouds and notice the glory that covers you, right where you are. Another option is to bring nature inside and fill your space with potted plants—even a little bit of green can work wonders.

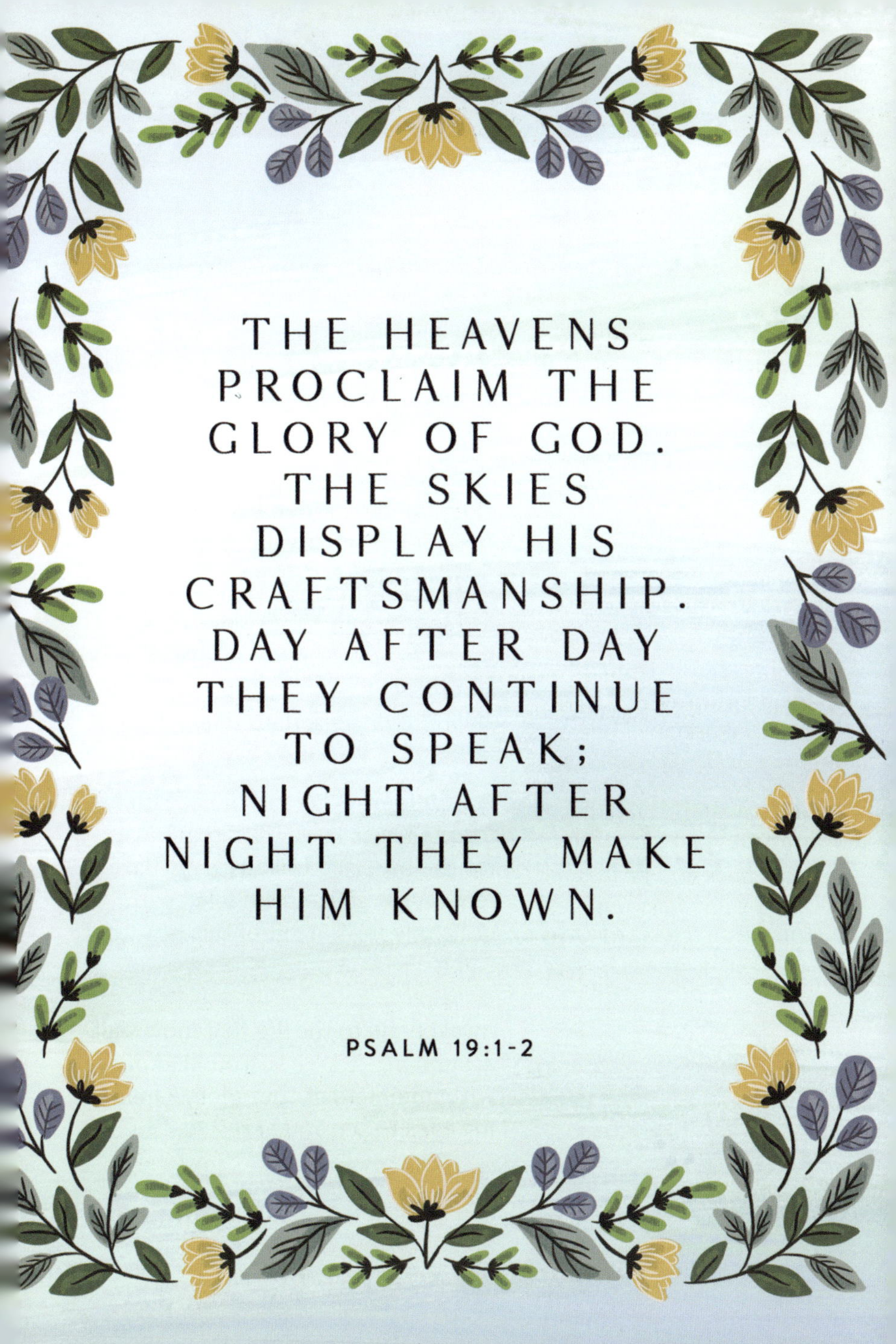
THE HEAVENS
PROCLAIM THE
GLORY OF GOD.
THE SKIES
DISPLAY HIS
CRAFTSMANSHIP.
DAY AFTER DAY
THEY CONTINUE
TO SPEAK;
NIGHT AFTER
NIGHT THEY MAKE
HIM KNOWN.
PSALM 19:1-2

EMBODIED PRAYER

Maker of sparrows and spruce trees,

Go outside (or look out a window if you are physically unable to go outside). Sit in the grass or on a bench, or walk along a path as you pray.

You have filled the earth with echoes of Eden, with beauty and wonder and so many good things.

All creation sings the song of Your glory. All the earth moves to the steady rhythm of Your grace.

Name as many things as you want, noticing any feelings that may arise as you pay attention to the world around you.

As I look around right now, I see ____________ (*name what you see*) and I feel ___________ (*consider the emotions or sensations that arise*).

Stretch your arms up like branches of a tree. Gently sway back and forth, take off your shoes, and feel the ground beneath your feet.

I stretch my arms and praise You for the trees. I sway and thank You for the breeze. I walk with my bare feet on the soil and am filled with gratitude for the gift of this beautiful earth.

Awaken me to the life that moves all around me. You've surrounded me with glimmers of Your glory. Open my eyes to see You here.

Amen.

AWAKEN ME

As you move and pray, turn your attention to the wonder of the world around you. Take time to notice something that you would normally just rush right by.

Take a slow walk outside, notice the butterflies, listen to the bird-song in the trees, smell a flower, watch the bees, feel the wind, reach down and touch the dirt, lay in the grass and watch the clouds, stand in the rain and feel the drops hit your skin, jump in a puddle, catch a snowflake and wonder at its design, watch a spider spinning its web, pick up a rock and feel its weight, watch the sunset, marvel at the stars.

There are so many ways to experience the world around you, to notice the fingerprints of God in everything He has made. He put so much intricate detail and care into the feathers of a bird and the leaves of a tree and the petals of a flower—just think how much more He cares for every detail of you!

The heavens proclaim the glory of God. The skies display his craftsmanship. Day after day they continue to speak; night after night they make him known.

PSALM 19:1–2

More grounding ideas

LET A PIECE OF CHOCOLATE MELT IN YOUR MOUTH

LOOK UP AND WATCH THE CLOUDS

HOLD AN ICE CUBE

PLANT YOUR BARE FEET ON THE EARTH

SPLASH COLD WATER ON YOUR FACE

WRAP YOURSELF IN A BLANKET

LIGHT A SCENTED CANDLE

SING!

HUG A PET

ACCEPT MY PRAYER
AS INCENSE OFFERED TO YOU,
AND MY UPRAISED HANDS
AS AN EVENING OFFERING.

PSALM 141:2

Movement Tools

In his book *God Walk*, Mark Buchanan wrote about the ways his prayer life has been influenced by the patriarch in the musical *Fiddler on the Roof*, Teras. He wrote how Teras "talks with God everywhere, face to face, friend to friend." He noted how these prayers are not done sitting but are prayed constantly as he is moving. Similar to Maewyn, whose story I shared earlier and who prayed a hundred times a day through every movement of his day, Teras's daily physical movements were a constant catalyst for prayer. Buchanan wrote, "It's almost as if movement triggers his praying, that his legs are connected, by strings and latches and pulleys, to his heart and mouth: once his legs engage, the other parts join in."[40]

We, too, can be moved to pray throughout our regular, ordinary days through simple movements. As we move, we begin to release stored-up stress, and as oxygen flows through our bloodstream, it brings life to our cells and we become primed for prayer. Our bodies become a moving and breathing vessel of embodied prayer. Buchanan describes it like this: "One step, two, and soon longing and gratitude and wonder and petition are working their way up through me, almost bodily, mingling with my thoughts, fusing with my emotions, pressing toward speech. Before long, all of it, the walking, the noticing, the feeling, the thinking, the speaking, is praying."[41]

Every movement can be an invitation to pray. Ordinary movements paired with embodied prayer help calm our body while deepening our connection to God and our sense of peace as we rest in His presence.

TAKE A MINDFUL WALK[42]

The simple act of walking can be a great tool to help you feel more present in your body. It helps reset your nervous system, balances your cortisol levels, and helps slow down your racing thoughts.[43]

Walking is a form of bilateral stimulation—movement that stimulates both hemispheres of the brain.[44] When you walk, you naturally move in a rhythmic way, alternating steps between your left and right feet as well as movements between your left and right arms. This bilateral movement helps your brain process and integrate information, which helps you process stress and move through emotions. It also activates the parasympathetic nervous system, which calms the body and increases serotonin and dopamine, which contribute to feelings of well-being.

We are usually distracted when we walk; our minds tend to wander to places other than where we are. We may listen to music or a podcast as we walk, or we may ruminate over things that have happened or worry about things to come. Mindful walking involves paying attention to the present moment as you move, noticing any sensations in your body or emotions the movements may bring up.

There's no need to walk quickly. This kind of walking is not about racing to finish fast or clocking any number of steps. This is about gently moving your body as you increase awareness of your sensations and emotions.

START WITH STILLNESS

Stand still for a moment before beginning your walk.

BREATHE

- Breathe intentionally and notice your regular breathing pattern.
- Try extending your inhale and exhale by a few seconds more than what comes naturally.
- Notice how your body feels as you slow down, and deepen your inhales and extend your exhales with more intention.
- Bring your breathing back to its normal rhythm.

FEEL

- Notice how the ground feels beneath your feet.
- Notice the firmness of the earth holding you up.

WALK

- Begin walking. Focus your attention on the sensations of your feet and legs moving through the air.
- Notice each step: the heel and the ball of the foot lifting, the toes coming off the ground, the body shifting weight, your foot and leg moving through space and then reconnecting with the earth.
- Notice how your legs rhythmically carry you.
- Notice how your arms sway as you move.
- Compassionately pay attention to any pain or discomfort you may be feeling.
- Try to focus on simply experiencing the sensations of walking without thinking about them or trying to change them. Simply notice your body as you walk.

PRAY

- Talk to God as you walk. Let the movement of your body move you closer to Him. Envision Him walking with you, right by your side. His presence is your constant companion.

LABYRINTH WALK

A labyrinth walk is a type of mindful walk. It is described by Jason and Dena Hobbs in their book, *When Anxiety Strikes*, as a walk that is "made for wandering."[45] It's not about going from point A to point B but about taking a winding, wandering way. If you have access to a labyrinth, that would be perfect for this activity. If not, you can walk your neighborhood or any area where you feel safe to wander.

Do not walk a straight path. Take turns you don't normally take. Go the long, meandering way.

BEGIN WITH THE BREATH

- Stand still and focus on taking a few deep breaths before you begin walking.
- Try extending your inhale and exhale by a few seconds more than what comes naturally.
- Notice how your body feels as you slow down; deepen your inhales and extend your exhales with more intention.
- Bring your breathing back to its normal rhythm.

FEEL

- Notice how the ground feels beneath your feet.
- Notice the firmness of the earth holding you up.

WALK

- Notice how your legs rhythmically carry you.
- Notice how your arms sway as you move.
- Try to focus on simply experiencing the sensations of walking without thinking about them or trying to change them. Simply notice your body as you walk.
- Notice new things along your route.
- Notice how you feel—your sensations and emotions—as you change the pattern of your normal path.

Go the slow way, the less efficient way, and pay attention to God's presence with you on the way.

> If walking is not an option for you, think of a way you could take the long, meandering way somewhere. Give yourself some extra time to wander as you drive on your way to work or school or the store, taking the less direct roads.

EMBODIED PRAYER

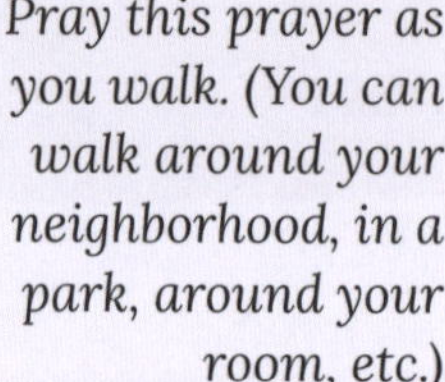

Pray this prayer as you walk. (You can walk around your neighborhood, in a park, around your room, etc.)

Walk slowly, paying attention to your steps and bringing your awareness to God's presence with you in this place.

Heavenly Father,

Walk with me along the way.
Examine my heart as I align my
pace with the rhythm of Your
grace, walking with You
step by step.

Show me what I need to release to
You—the stress, the pain, the
worries, the fears.

I won't rush. I won't hurry.

Step by step, I will walk with You.
Step by step, I will listen for Your voice.
Step by step, I will notice Your goodness.
Step by step, I will enjoy Your presence.

I give You the hard things I am carrying.
I trust You to keep making a way through.

As I move toward You, may hope move like
a sweet relief through me and fill me with
Your peace.

Amen.

STEP BY STEP

As you move and pray, pay attention to the pace of your day. Are you rushing through your moments? Is your body always busy or your mind always racing as you jump from one task to the next?

The truth is, we live in a noisy and fast-paced world with packed schedules and little breathing room. Our days quickly fill with chores and errands, cooking and cleaning, work and school, kids and family. It's so very easy to get swept away in the never-ending flow of demands and pressure to accomplish more.

What would it look like to slow down, even just a little bit? What would it look like to take just one step at a time, one moment at a time, and give that moment your complete attention? Invite God to walk with you today, and move at the pace of His grace, keeping your senses awakened to all that He has for you in the small and ordinary moments of your life.

O Lord, you have examined my heart and know everything about me. . . You know everything I do.
PSALM 139:1–3

SOMATIC STRETCHING

Somatic stretching involves gentle movements that can help release muscular tension and increase your mind-body awareness. This type of stretching isn't so much about pulling or stretching the muscles as it is about slowing down and tuning in to how your muscles feel, then contracting and relaxing them to release tension and increase mobility. As you become more aware of how your muscles feel, you'll be able to recognize more easily when parts of your body are feeling tighter than usual, cueing you to any underlying stress or emotional overwhelm you may be storing in your body.

For each of these stretches:

- Find a comfortable and quiet space.
- Close your eyes and pay attention to your body.
- Move slowly and gently, listening to your body's cues.
- Hold each stretch for several breaths.
- As you stretch, pay attention to how you are feeling. Be present in the moment and remind your soul that God is there with you.
- Pray to the rhythm of the gentle movements, giving thanks to God for the body He gave you.

Try different stretches to see what feels most comfortable to you. These movements should not be painful. If you have any injuries, please consult a medical professional before attempting any new movements.

HANG YOUR HEAD[46]

This somatic movement benefits the neck and shoulders.

- Stand straight with your feet on the floor.
- Slowly hang your head, letting it fall as far down as it will comfortably go.
- Notice how your neck muscles feel.
- Notice how the movement affects your shoulders, upper back, and other nearby muscles, joints, and tissues.
- Identify any tense areas, such as the back of your neck, and really experience how that tension feels.
- Notice how it feels to settle into the stretch, and try to release some of the tension.

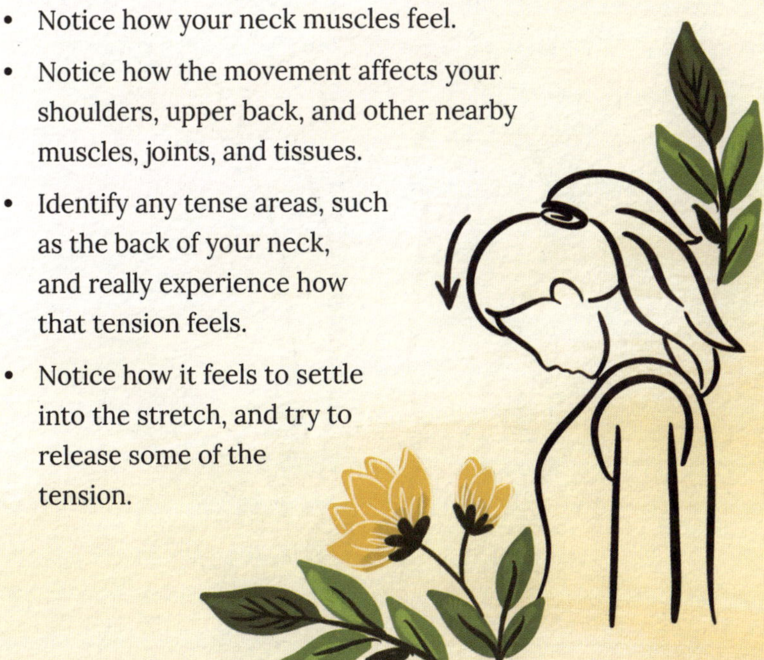

FORWARD BEND

This stretch is a standing pose that releases tension in the neck, shoulders, and back.

- Stand with your feet hip-width apart.
- Slowly bend forward at the hips, letting your arms hang toward the ground.
- Allow your head to hang heavy, releasing any strain on your neck.
- Stay in this position for a few breaths, then slowly roll back up to a standing position.

SEATED SIDE BEND

This movement stretches the sides of the body—including the hips, spine, and torso—and helps improve flexibility, balance, and range of motion.

- Sit cross-legged with a straight back.
- Place your right palm on the floor near your hip.
- Inhale, then raise your left arm out to the side and up above your head.
- Exhale, then slide your right hand across the floor out to the right.
- Bend to the right, keeping your buttocks on the floor.
- Inhale to return to an upright position.
- Repeat on the other side.

CROCODILE STRETCH

This is a resting pose that can help relieve stress, tension in the lower back, and open up your chest and shoulders.

- Lie on your stomach with your forearms stacked above your head, then rest your forehead on your wrists. You may find it more comfortable to use a prop or blanket to rest your head on.
- Let your body sink into the floor and take deep, circular breaths that fill up your abdomen, pelvis, back, and ribs.
- Avoid looking upward or tilting your head back, as this may strain your neck or put pressure on your lower back.

ARCH AND FLATTEN[47]

This movement helps release tension in the lower back.

- Lie on your back and position your feet flat on the floor, hip-distance apart, with your knees bent.
- Take a deep breath, noticing how the muscles in your lower back and abdomen move as you do.
- Gently arch your back, bringing your belly upward and pressing your glute muscles and feet into the floor.
- Stay here for as long as feels comfortable, then slowly lower your back and flatten it against the floor.
- Repeat the movement very slowly, scanning the muscles in your torso for any tension, trying to release that tension.

ILIOPSOAS EXERCISE[48]

Brings awareness to the iliopsoas, the muscle group that attaches your spine to your legs.

- Lie on your back with your knees bent, feet flat on the floor.
- Place your right hand behind your head.
- Gently lift your head as you simultaneously lift your right leg, keeping it bent, about six inches off the floor. (This should look a bit like you're doing a crunch with just one side of your body.)
- Scan the muscles in your lower back, hips, and legs for tension, noticing how they feel.
- Gently lower your leg and head.
- Do it again, this time straightening your leg slightly as you lift.
- Repeat these motions slowly and gently several times, then do the same on the other side.

RECLINED TWIST

This movement stretches the spine and encourages relaxation through the core.

- Lie on your back with your knees bent.
- Gently lower both knees to one side, keeping your shoulders flat on the ground.
- Hold this position for a few breaths, feeling the stretch along your spine.
- Bring your knees back to the center, then repeat on the other side.

LEGS UP

This gentle resting pose can help alleviate lower back pain and improve circulation, best performed in a quiet spot at home, away from distractions.

- Sit with your side against a wall, your knees bent and feet drawn in toward your hips.
- Swing your legs up against the wall as you turn to lie flat on your back.
- Place your hips against the wall or slightly away as you extend your legs up the wall, allowing your feet to rest against it.
- Relax your arms in any position that's comfortable.
- Close your eyes and stay in the pose for two to twenty minutes.

An alternative option would be to use a chair instead of a wall: Lie on the floor with your knees bent and your calves and feet resting up on the seat of a chair.

EMBODIED PRAYER

As you pray, move your body in slow and gentle patterns, whatever is comfortable for you. You can gently sway as you let your arms softly swing. You can walk in slow circles, stepping to the rhythm of your prayer. You could even move your hands, opening your palms to give God your fears and receive His love.

God of hope,

Renew my strength today as I move in faith.

Move hope through my body as I move my muscles to the rhythm of Your grace.
Move hope through my soul as I turn my awareness toward You and the safety of Your presence.

Strengthen my connection to You and secure me deeply in Your abiding love.

All the stress and pain and trauma I hold—You see it all, and You hold it all with me.
I am not alone.

Today, I will move and I will let hope move through me.

I give You my weakness.
I lay my fears at Your feet.
Strengthen me in Your love.

Amen.

LET HOPE MOVE

As you move and pray, open your heart to the hope that God has for you today.

Depending on your circumstances, it may not be easy to recognize the gift of your body or feel the goodness in your body right now, and that's ok. But what if you began to believe that even here, in the middle of your deepest pain and discomfort, God is with you? Even here, your body is working hard to protect you, to keep you safe, to help you survive. Even in the midst of deep suffering, your body invites you to listen to the story it is telling, to respond with curiosity and self-compassion, to accept the care and the nourishment you need, to rest in God and depend on others and find hope in knowing you are not alone.

Every movement you make is a movement of hope as you trust that God is working beneath the surface in ways you can't even imagine right now. He is with you, even now.

He gives strength to the weary
and increases the power of the weak.
ISAIAH 40:29 NIV

HALF SUN SALUTE[49]

My friends, Jason and Dena Hobbs, shared this Half Sun Salute exercise in their book, *When Anxiety Strikes*, and it has become one of my favorites for helping me reconnect with my body through movement while also connecting to God through prayer.

- Stand with your feet slightly apart and your arms at your sides.
- Inhale as you lift your hands over your head.
- Exhale as you tilt back slightly into a standing backbend. (Only bend as far as is comfortable for you.)
- Hold this pose and take a deep breath with your heart open and hands uplifted to God.
- On your next inhale, stand upright again with your arms stretched up and hands open.
- Exhale as you roll forward, bending down as if touching your toes.
- Let the crown of your head drop down.
- Hold this bowed position and take a deep breath.
- On your next inhale, roll back up and stand with your hands lifted overhead.
- Finish with an exhale as you rest your hands folded together over your heart in a prayer position.

Pray a prayer of
praise as you raise
your arms in the air.

Pray a prayer of
humble supplication
as you bow.

Repeat these movements as you pray to God.

PROGRESSIVE MUSCLE RELAXATION

In this exercise, muscle groups are intentionally tensed and then relaxed.

Repeat each step at least once, holding the tensed muscles for five to seven seconds before releasing for fifteen to thirty seconds. Pay attention to the contrast of sensations between tension and relaxation.

1. ARMS & HANDS

Curl both fists, tightening biceps and forearms.
Hold.
Relax.

2. SHOULDERS

Arch your shoulders back as you take a deep breath into your chest.
Hold.
Relax.

3. HEAD

Roll your head around on your neck clockwise in a complete circle, then reverse.
Hold.
Relax.
Wrinkle up the muscles of your face like a walnut: forehead wrinkled, eyes squinted, mouth opened, and shoulders hunched.
Hold.
Relax.

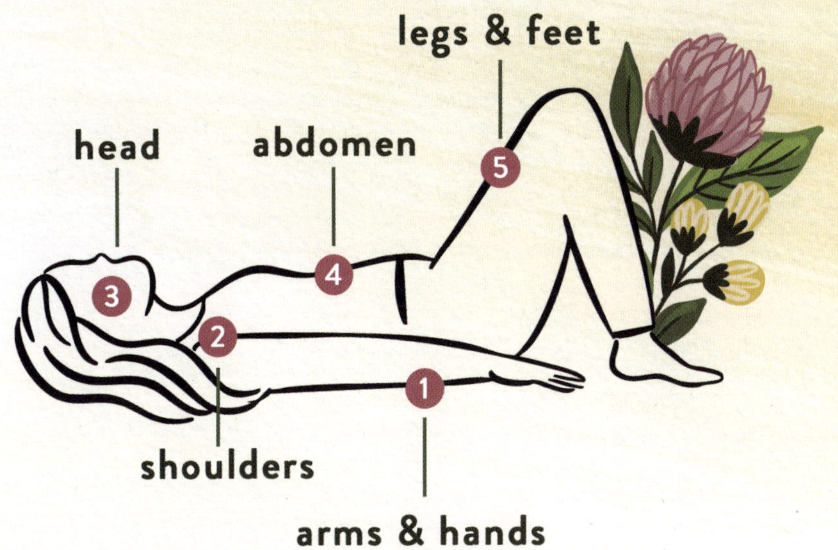

4. ABDOMEN

Take a deep breath, pushing out your stomach.

Hold.

Relax.

5. LEGS & FEET

Straighten your legs and point your toes back toward your face, tightening your shins.

Hold.

Relax.

Straighten your legs and curl your toes, simultaneously tightening your calves, thighs, and buttocks.

Hold.

Relax.

PAIRED MUSCLE RELAXATION

Paired Muscle Relaxation is similar to Progressive Muscle Relaxation in that you are systematically tensing and releasing your muscles. With this version, you are also pairing those movements with your breath. You will tense your muscles as you inhale and then relax them as you exhale.

ARMS & HANDS

Inhale as you tighten your fists and tense your arm muscles.
Hold.
Exhale as you relax your hands and arms.

SHOULDERS

Inhale as you arch your shoulders back.
Hold.
Exhale as you release and relax your shoulders.

HEAD

Inhale as you tighten the muscles in your face.
Hold.
Exhale as you relax your face.

ABDOMEN

Inhale as you tighten your abdominal muscles.
Hold.
Exhale as you relax your stomach.

LEGS

Inhale as you stretch out your legs and tighten your leg muscles.
Hold.
Exhale as you relax your legs.

Pair your breath and muscle movement with an anchor prayer like this one to connect your heart to God and His peace as you gently move.

inhale:

FILL ME WITH YOUR PEACE.

exhale:

I GIVE YOU ALL MY WORRIES.

EMBODIED PRAYER

God of peace,

If you are physically able, get down on your knees, then bend forward and lower your head as far down toward the floor as is comfortable.

I kneel before You now.

I bow down in Your presence, remembering that You are with me.

Reach your arms out in front of you as you are bowed on the floor.

I reach for You, with my arms and with my heart, remembering that You love me.

Take slow, deep breaths as you focus on the presence of God.

I breathe deeply in this place, remembering that You are watching over me.

I am safe here, in Your loving care. Help me rest in You, my Lord and my God.

Amen.

SAFE IN HIS CARE

As you move and pray, turn your heart and mind to the presence of God and His loving care for you in every moment.

Our bodies are made to seek safety. Some of us seek safety in cultivating cozy and calm spaces; some of us seek it in slowness and stillness; some of us seek it in comforting relationships or satisfying experiences. But life is messy. And not every moment of every day can be calming candles and warm blankets. True peace must come from a foundation of safety that is rooted deeper than any feelings we may feel and any coziness we concoct. We need something that sustains through the dark and difficult days, through the deepest pain and trauma, and through all the heartbreaks and aches of this life. And that something is actually a someone—the One who is Peace: Jesus Christ.

You are fully loved and fully accepted by God. Just as you are.

What would life in your body be like if you lived from a place of complete acceptance and security that is grounded in God's abiding and unchanging love and care for you?

We are the people he watches over, the flock under his care.

PSALM 95:7

SHAKE IT OUT

Shaking helps release stress hormones and calms the body. This is particularly helpful following a stressful event, as it will allow your body to release excess energy and regulate the nervous system.

Similar to the way animals typically get up and shake themselves vigorously after surviving a predator attack, "We complete the stress cycle," Hillary L. McBride writes, "when we release our trauma response mechanisms by moving the stress-related energy out through the body. This often happens involuntarily, through shaking, but we can help ourselves by doing it on purpose—by running, dancing, wiggling, jumping, or squeezing our muscles for a few moments with all our might."[50]

GIVE IT A TRY!

- Bend your knees slightly and, with both feet firmly planted on the floor, begin slowly bouncing up and down.
- Let your shoulders, belly, and hands relax as you shake.
- Shake for five to fifteen minutes, or however long is comfortable, focusing on how your body feels as you move.
- Notice the weight of your own body and the sensation of breathing in and out while shaking.

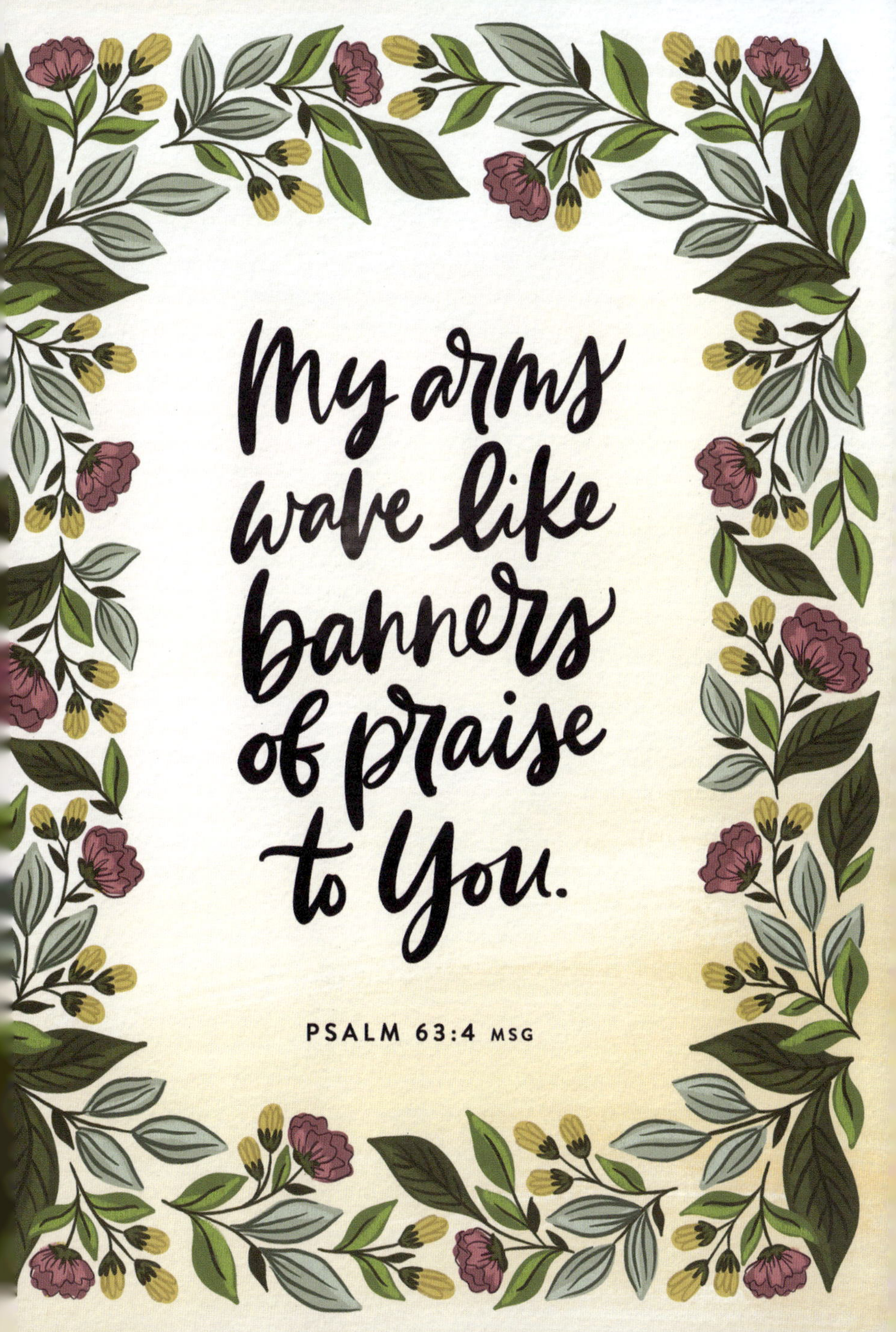
My arms wave like banners of praise to You.
PSALM 63:4 MSG

PLAY

When we are feeling overwhelmed or stressed, or feeling symptoms of anxiety or depression, we often lose our sense of playfulness. Laughter leaves and everything feels heavy.

Play helps to lighten our spirits. Play connects us to our body in a fun and unstructured way. Laughter literally stimulates the vagus nerve, which helps our nervous system to regulate and promotes a sense of calm.[51] Play is a kind of movement that is all about joy. We're not moving to change our body; we're moving to *enjoy* our body.

But this can be challenging if you haven't played in a long time. Consider:

- What did you do for play when you were a child?
- What did you enjoy most as a child?
- What did you become so absorbed in that you lost track of time?
- What made you feel free?
- Those activities are a good clue to the kinds of activities that will be playful for you today.
- Is there anything you can try now?

If you're not sure, try something that sounds fun to you and see how you feel. If you are enjoying yourself, you've got it! If you're not having fun, then try something else. Remember, the point is not to be good at it or to get some kind of result. This is all about finding joy in enjoying your body through play.

PLAY
A CARD
GAME
JUMP ON A BED
OR TRAMPOLINE
PLAY
A SPORT
PLANT A
GARDEN
play!
PLAY A
BOARD
GAME
PAINT
OR DRAW
CROCHET OR KNIT
SOMETHING
PLAY
HOPSCOTCH
MAKE SILLY FACES
IN A MIRROR

Praise his name with dancing...

PSALM 149:3

CREATIVE EXPRESSION

Express yourself creatively through movement. Pick up a paintbrush, a pen, a ribbon, or some clay, and let your body express your feelings or emotions creatively. Engaging in creative movement can be therapeutic, helping you release tension, manage stress, and boost your mood.[52] Even if you don't think you're a naturally creative person, you may be surprised by what you create when you let go of judgment and expectations and simply allow yourself to enjoy the process. Start small with a creative activity that interests you, and focus on how you feel as you engage in that activity. Remember, creative expression is not about creating a perfect end result. It's about the joy of the process and allowing your emotions to flow through your creative expression.

- Dancing
- Coloring
- Crafting/DIY projects
- Painting
- Twirling around a ribbon or a scarf
- Playing an instrument
- Sculpting
- Writing
- Photography

NATURE-INSPIRED MOVEMENT

This is a fluid, imaginative exercise inspired by the movements found in the world around us. All of creation is full of movement—clouds floating across the sky, fish swimming in the sea, squirrels scurrying on the ground, the rise and fall of the tides, the swift flow of the rivers, and the slow growth of flowers. Movement is all around us. Experience a bit of freedom and fun in your movements by moving like the plants and animals in nature. If you have children, this could be a fun activity to do together. Here are some ideas to get you started:

SWAY IN THE WIND Imagine you're a sunflower swaying in a gentle breeze.

STRETCH AND REACH Emulate the stretching of a plant's roots toward water or a shoot toward sunlight.

MIMIC THE OPENING AND CLOSING OF FLOWERS Explore movements that mimic the opening and closing of flowers like tulips in response to temperature changes.

MOVE LIKE A SEA CREATURE Move your arms and legs like you're swimming in the ocean. Pretend you have tentacles or fins. Let your arms move freely as you swirl and sway in the water.

WALK LIKE A BEAR Move on your hands and feet without letting your knees touch the floor.

MOVE LIKE A BIRD OR BUTTERFLY Move your arms up and down like a bird or butterfly flying through the air.

What other animals or plants or movements of the earth can you mimic in your movements?

EMBODIED PRAYER

As you pray this prayer of praise, move freely in a way that brings you joy! You can dance, shake, sway . . . Move in any way that is comfortable and enjoyable for you.

Heavenly Father,

I may be carrying grief or shame or fear
or worry and I may be in the midst of
sadness or pain, deep
discouragement or despair.
But right now in this moment,
I'm choosing to experience joy!

I dance before You, a defiant act of joy.

Let hope flow through me as I dance.
Let joy flow through me as I move.
Let Your grace fill all my hurting places
Let Your love cover all my fears.

I dance before You, Lord.
I praise You with my whole self.
In Your loving presence, my sorrow
shares space with gladness, and my
weeping holds hands with joy.

Amen.

MOVE WITH JOY

As you move and pray, pay attention to how you feel in your body right now. In what ways can you experience joy in your body?

Your body is a good body. This doesn't mean that every experience in your body is good. And it is not meant to be a mantra of toxic positivity, or a means of spiritual bypassing and ignoring the very real and significant impact pain and trauma may have on your life. It is instead an invitation to gently shift your bodily orientation away from shame and self-loathing and toward an orientation of hope—hope that God is working in and through your right-now body, inviting you to connect and commune with Him, to experience goodness and beauty and joy in this life, and to lead you to places of safety and peace as you move through your days in prayerful communication with Him and in mindful awareness of His constant presence with you through it all.

Your body is a good body. So go ahead and shake and dance and move with joy! God is with you and you are so very loved!

You have turned my mourning into joyful dancing. You have taken away my clothes of mourning and clothed me with joy.

PSALM 30:11

More Movement ideas
JOG IN PLACE
GARDEN
TOSS AND CATCH A BALLOON
JUMP UP AND DOWN
DO LEG LIFTS FROM A CHAIR
RIDE A BICYCLE
STOMP YOUR FEET
TAP RHYTHMICALLY ON A SURFACE

THE WAY GOD DESIGNED
OUR BODIES IS A MODEL
FOR UNDERSTANDING
OUR LIVES TOGETHER
AS A CHURCH:
EVERY PART DEPENDENT
ON EVERY OTHER PART.

1 CORINTHIANS 12:25 MSG

Connection Tools

We weren't made to move through life alone. There is safety, healing, strength, and peace in connection—connection to ourselves, connection to others, and connection to God. God's design—both for our individual bodies and for the collective body of Christ, His church—is for connection and unity.

Connections are important for our mental and physical health. Staying connected to others creates feelings of being loved, cared for, and valued. Connecting with others can help regulate our nervous system and give us a sense of safety and belonging. Connection is the key to living a truly flourishing, abundant life.

The human body is designed for connection and togetherness. But it is also designed to withdraw from anything it perceives as unsafe. If you've experienced harm, neglect, or disappointment from others, it may be difficult to seek out connection. It is our natural tendency to withdraw in order to protect ourselves. Over time, this can get us stuck in patterns of protection and make it difficult to develop patterns of connection. If connecting with others feels unsafe to you, please take this process slowly.

Start by asking yourself:

- When and where do I feel most safe to be myself?
- With whom is it easiest for me to connect?

Start slow. Start small. Begin where it feels safe and tolerable and expand slowly from there. This is not an all-or-nothing practice, but a practice in gradually expanding your circle of safety and connection over time.

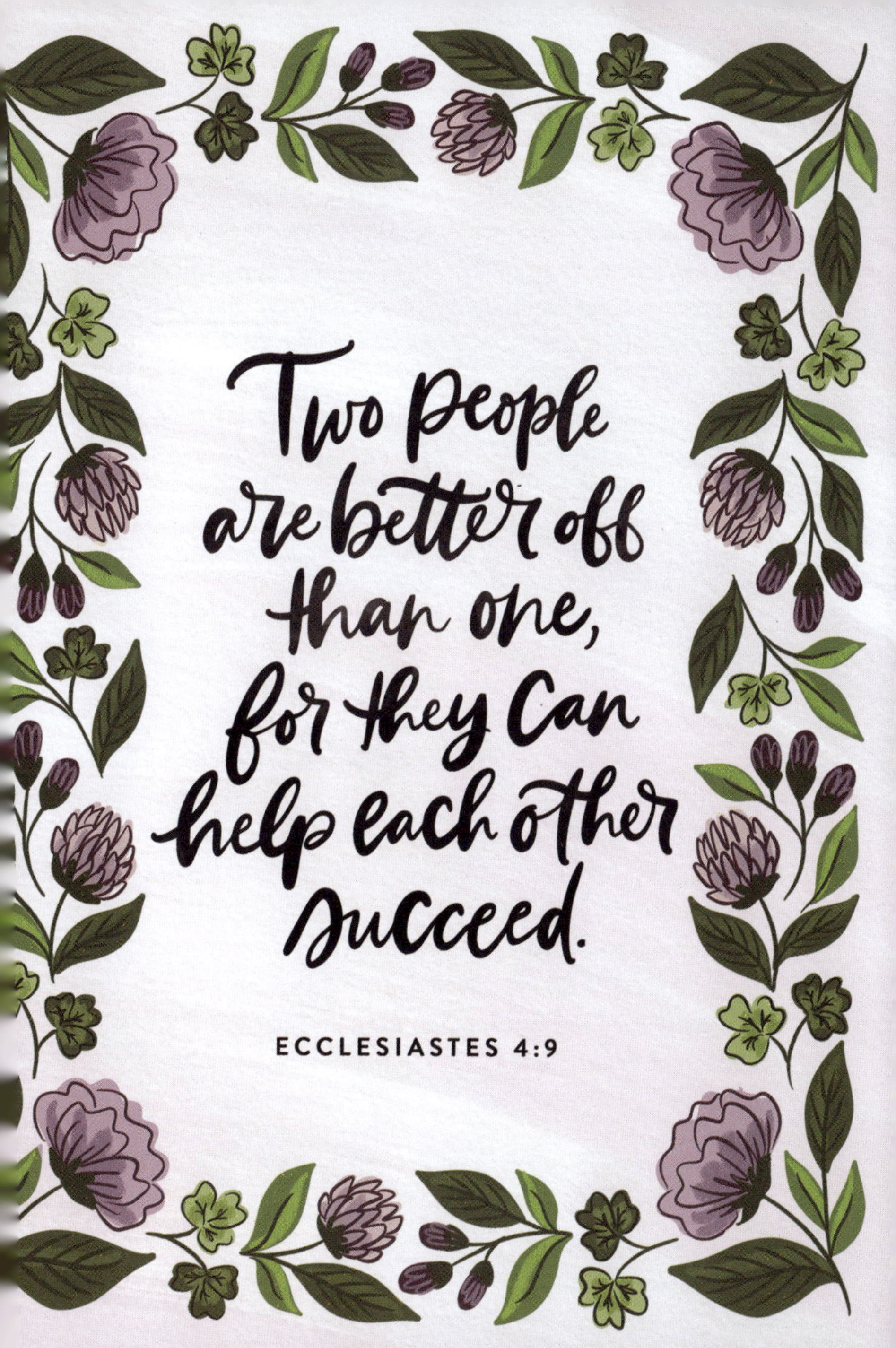
Two people
are better off
than one,
for they can
help each other
succeed.
ECCLESIASTES 4:9

CO-REGULATION

Co-regulation is the term used to describe when two people come together to help each other navigate and regulate their emotions, creating a supportive emotional environment.

Co-regulation plays an important role in helping children develop the ability to manage distressing sensations and emotions. When reliable and nurturing caregivers are able to pay close attention to their children's emotional and physiological cues and provide supportive, consistent responses in the midst of distress, while also regulating their own emotional states, children develop a growing capacity for self-regulation.[53]

Even as adults, co-regulation is beneficial in all kinds of relationships, including romantic relationships, friendships, and even relationships between coworkers. During stressful times, there's a shared effort to address and alleviate emotional distress. In moments of joy, there's shared happiness and connection. It is a process where emotional support is mutual, and it can lead to deeper connections, improved emotional regulation, and enhanced resilience.[54]

Sometimes—and even more so as we learn and practice self-regulation—we can handle our stress on our own, and a little "self-care" is all we need. But many times we also need community care. We need support from each other. Our bodies are made to help one another calm and heal within a safe and compassionate environment.

SHARING JOY
SUPPORTING THROUGH STRESS
CELEBRATING SUCCESSES
OFFERING EMPATHY
COMMUNICATING CLEARLY
Co-regulation
CAN LOOK LIKE:
ACTIVE LISTENING
SHARING POSITIVE EXPERIENCES
PHYSICAL TOUCH
(hug, pat on the back, holding hands)
CHECKING IN WITH EACH OTHER
GOING FOR A WALK TOGETHER
ACKNOWLEDGING FEELINGS & VALIDATING EMOTIONS

MIRRORING

Mirroring is an activity that can be done with someone you trust and feel safe with. If we're disconnected from our body in some way, we may not be fully aware of how we carry and display our emotions. This activity helps us see from another perspective, which can give us some insight into how we hold our emotions. This is a great activity you can even practice with your kids to teach them various emotions and help them learn to become aware of the emotions they feel, what those emotions look like, and how their bodies express those emotions. Helping kids develop emotional awareness early can have a significant impact on their emotional regulation as they grow.

- Stand or sit across from one another.
- One person embodies an emotion, expressing that emotion in their face and/or body in whatever way is typical for them.
- The other person "mirrors" them and does exactly what they are doing, reflecting back to them the emotions they're seeing on their face and how they're holding their body.

Take turns practicing a variety of emotions, mirroring one another's embodiment of the various feelings.

SOME FEELINGS TO TRY MIRRORING

afraid, amazed, angry, annoyed, anxious, ashamed, confident, confused, delighted, depressed, disgusted, excited, exhausted, frustrated, happy, hurt, miserable, nervous, peaceful, sad, shy, surprised, unsure, upset.

EMBODIED PRAYER

For this prayer, pray with someone you know (a spouse, a friend, etc.). Join hands if that feels safe and comfortable.

Alternate praying for one another, sharing needs and offering compassion and comfort. Add your own words as you pray, personalizing the prayer for one another. This may feel a bit awkward, but it is good for us to carry one another's burdens and to commune with God together—the One who unites us all through His Spirit within us.

Alternatively, you can pray this prayer alone for someone in your life. Hold them in your mind and bring them before God as you pray. You can stretch your hands out with your palms up as you offer this prayer, or place your hands over your heart.

God of us all,

(Pray for the other person, then switch and have the other person pray the same prayer for you.)

Thank You for __________ *(name).* He/She is a blessing to me because ____________.

In their life, I see a reflection of Your _________ *(love, joy, patience, goodness, grace, mercy, kindness, etc.).*

I know he/she is carrying ________ *(pain, fear, worry, grief, sorrow, disappointment).* Write Your love into their story and help them see glimmers of Your goodness, filling all their aching places with Your peace.

Show me how I can embody Your love in their life in practical and compassionate ways, reminding them they are not alone.

Help us bear each other's burdens and share each other's joys. You didn't create us to be alone in this world. You designed us to need each other.

Thank You for the gift of ______________________ *(name).*

Amen.

A PRAYER FOR ONE ANOTHER

As you move and pray, consider the ways you typically seek or avoid connection in your life.

Our souls were made to seek meaningful connection, but too often we settle for online distraction that only leaves us ultimately feeling disconnected and isolated from our own feelings and the actual lives of others. We weren't meant to live in a bubble. Our lives were always meant to intersect with one another. The truth is, we need each other. We never meant to go it alone.

Prayer can be a powerful conduit to deeper connection, not only to God but also to yourself and to others. God moves and works in all of our lives, and He gives us one another to embody His love and care in each other's lives. When you pray with someone and carry their burdens with them to the feet of Jesus, you get to experience the beauty and joy that come from a genuine connection flowing from His faithful love that unites us all.

God works in different ways, but it is the same
God who does the work in all of us.

1 CORINTHIANS 12:6

PARTNER MOVEMENT

You can deepen your connection to another person when you join in some kind of movement together. When you move together, you offer one another social support as well as companionship, which can help boost your mood, increase self-efficacy, and keep you motivated to make movement a regular habit. Do something that you both enjoy, and focus on being fully present in the moment.

SOME THINGS YOU CAN DO TOGETHER:

- Take a walk.
- Take a dance class.
- Do a puzzle.
- Play a sport.
- Go boating on the lake.
- Go on a hike.
- Go birdwatching.
- Go for a drive.
- Play a board game.
- Bake some goodies to share.

Carry each other's burdens...

GALATIANS 6:2 NIV

LISTEN TO YOUR LONELINESS

While connection is key to a more flourishing life, disconnection—whether through social isolation or feelings of loneliness—can have a withering effect on your life, putting you at greater risk of developing serious mental and physical health conditions.[55] Loneliness and isolation can feel like a heaviness or lack of energy and can negatively impact your self-worth. Chronic loneliness substantially increases the risk of heart disease, stroke, diabetes, depression, anxiety, dementia, and even the way you perceive pain. It also raises the risk of early death.[56]

Times of solitude are not entirely negative, and being alone can often be a healthy, positive choice that can help reduce stress and benefit your mental and spiritual health, giving you space to connect with God and with yourself.[57] Loneliness is not about being physically alone, but about feeling socially disconnected. Even those who enjoy times of solitude still need to connect with others.

Unfortunately, disconnection is common in our connected-online-but-disconnected-in-person world. About one in three adults in the US report feeling lonely, and one in four adults report not having social and emotional support.[58] Loneliness is all around us. Pay attention to any feelings of disconnection or loneliness you may be experiencing, and begin to look for the signs of loneliness in others. We were made for connection. Let loneliness act as a reminder to move toward greater connection. It can be something as simple as sending a text, offering a smile, or meeting a friend for coffee. Even little glimmers of connection can remind us we're not alone.

MOVE TOWARD Connection

- Ask a friend to join you for a task you usually do solo, like walking the dog or grocery shopping.
- Say "hi" to people on the sidewalk.
- Chat with someone in line at the store.
- Volunteer in your community.
- Invite someone over for dinner or a game night.
- Send a simple text, like "I was just thinking about you and wanted to say hi."
- Do random acts of kindness.
- Join a Bible study group.
- Ask for help.
- Ask a checkout clerk, "How's your day?"
- Go to church.
- Sign up for a class at a library, museum, or other community venue.
- Make cookies for a neighbor.
- Check in on a friend or relative who lives alone.
- Write a thank-you note or email to let someone know how much of a difference they make in your life.

EMBODIED PRAYER

Jesus, God incarnate,

Sit or kneel in a comfortable position.

I praise Your holy name!
You do not love us from afar.

Raise your arms, hands extended toward the sky. Lower your arms, hands extended toward the ground.

Clothed in humanity,
You took on the form of a man
And embodied all that it means to be human.
You know what it is to feel joy and pain,
To grow and to learn,
To laugh and to cry,
To live and to die.

Fold your arms across your chest. Feel your heartbeat with your hands. (Just think: Jesus had a heartbeat like you!)

It's a profound and beautiful mystery—
How You made us all in the likeness of You, And You came to earth in the likeness of us—
All for connection,
All for communion,
All to come close to us—
To be God with us
And to be God for us.

Repeat the movements of raised arms, lowered arms, and folded arms in whatever rhythm feels comfortable for you.

As I follow in Your way, may I embody all that it means to be like You, my embodied Savior—to serve and give and help and embrace and comfort and love with my whole self, body and soul.

Amen.

LIKE JESUS

As you move and pray, turn your focus toward Jesus. Consider the incarnation—how God became flesh, and how Jesus was born as a baby and lived in a body just like yours and mine. Consider how God made you in His image for the purpose of relationship, so that you can know Him and be known by Him.

We were made by His love, formed to find safety in His love, created to connect to His love, and divinely designed to reflect the image of Love Himself. Living a full life in Christ means living like Jesus—fully embodied. We are called to reflect our embodied Christ who loved with His whole self, who touched the eyes of the blind and knelt down on His knees with the sick, who held children in His arms and was filled with compassion for the people He saw, who knelt and prayed, feasted and celebrated, listened and helped, suffered and mourned.

How are you living a whole-body faith like Jesus did?

So the Word became human and made his home among us. He was full of unfailing love and faithfulness. And we have seen his glory, the glory of the Father's one and only Son.

JOHN 1:14

SAY A PRAYER OF BLESSING

There's an exercise in mindfulness practice that is centered on extending loving-kindness to others. This involves simply holding someone in your mind and focusing on loving thoughts toward them. It could be someone in your family or neighborhood, or someone from work or church—anyone can be the focus of your loving-kindness.

As Christians, we have an even more powerful tool available to us: prayer. We know that God hears our prayers, and praying for someone is one way we can show love and deepen our connection to others and to God. Praying for others can also help turn our attention away from ourselves as we extend compassion to others. Sometimes, if we aren't careful, mindfulness and awareness practices can cause us to focus only on ourselves, but care for ourselves should ultimately lead us to extend care to others. When we are in a grounded and secure place emotionally, we are better able to reach out with unhindered compassion toward the people around us. Taking time to focus on others increases our empathy, enables us to see past our own struggles and circumstances, and helps us recognize that every person is going through their own set of hard things.

To practice prayerful loving-kindness toward others, try praying a prayer of blessing over someone.

- Think of an individual person. This could be someone who asked you to pray for them or someone you know who needs God's love and peace right now.
- Close your eyes and picture their face.
- Visualize what they may be doing right now and bring awareness to God's presence with them in this moment, just as He is present with you.
- Say a prayer of blessing for them. You can use one of the blessings found in Scripture, or pray a prayer with your own words. Ask God to bless them in specific ways.

BLESSINGS FROM SCRIPTURE

The Lord bless you and keep you;
the Lord make his face shine on you
and be gracious to you;
the Lord turn his face toward you
and give you peace.
NUMBERS 6:24–26 NIV

May the God of hope
fill you with all joy and peace
as you trust in him,
so that you may overflow with hope
by the power of the Holy Spirit.
ROMANS 15:13 NIV

Now may the God of peace—
who brought up from the dead our Lord Jesus,
the great Shepherd of the sheep,
and ratified an eternal covenant with his blood—
may he equip you with all you need for doing his will.
May he produce in you, through the power of Jesus Christ, every
good thing that is pleasing to him.
All glory to him forever and ever!
Amen.
HEBREWS 13:20–21

May the grace of the Lord Jesus Christ, the love of God,
and the fellowship of the Holy Spirit be with you all.
2 CORINTHIANS 13:14

I pray that from his glorious, unlimited resources
he will empower you with inner strength
through his Spirit.
Then Christ will make his home in your hearts
as you trust in him.
Your roots will grow down into God's love
and keep you strong.
And may you have the power to understand,
as all God's people should,
how wide, how long, how high,
and how deep his love is.
May you experience the love of Christ,
though it is too great to understand fully.
Then you will be made complete
with all the fullness of life
and power that comes from God.
EPHESIANS 3:16–19

Now may the Lord of peace himself
give you his peace at all
times and in every situation.
The Lord be with you all.
2 THESSALONIANS 3:16

EMBODIED WORSHIP

A woman in the town who was a sinner found out that Jesus was reclining at the table in the Pharisee's house. She brought an alabaster jar of perfume and stood behind him at his feet, weeping, and began to wash his feet with her tears. She wiped his feet with her hair, kissing them and anointing them with the perfume.

LUKE 7:37–38 CSB

This passage is a beautiful picture of embodied worship. Without a word, this woman, who was so moved by the overwhelming mercy and grace of forgiveness that she received, knelt down on her knees and poured out her love for Jesus through her hands and her hair and her tears and her lips. This humble act of honor and love engaged all the senses, from the scent of the perfume that filled the air to the sound of her tears falling on His feet. Every movement of her hands was an act of prayerful worship for her Lord, every kiss an expression of her love and gratitude. This embodied act of worship was pleasing to the Lord.

We, too, are invited to bless God with our bodies as we worship and praise Him. Clapping, raising your hands, bowing, kneeling, weeping, lifting your eyes, playing instruments, singing, dancing, and even lying down on the ground are all postures of worship. These are all movements that our bodies can do to express praise and glory and honor to God.

Worship is not just singing a few songs during a church service. Paul clearly states in Romans 12:1 that we are to offer our whole bodies to God in worship: "Therefore, I urge you, brothers and sisters, in view of God's mercy, to offer your bodies as a living sacrifice, holy and pleasing to God—this is your true and proper worship" (NIV).

True worship is lived and embodied as we walk through every moment of our days and "live a life worthy of the calling you have received" (Ephesians 4:1 NIV).

When we live in and for Christ—with awareness of His presence, gratitude for His goodness, communion with His Spirit, compassion for His creation—movement becomes a living, breathing act of worship.

How can you worship God with your movements today?

EMBODIED PRAYER

Heavenly Father,

Inhale as you lift your arms into the air, stretching up toward the sun. Breathe deeply as you pray words of praise to God.

I praise You for . . .

Exhale as you bow your head and bend forward, stretching your arms down toward the ground. Breathe deeply as you pray words of supplication to God.

Repeat as many times as you want, raising your arms in praise, and bowing down in supplication.

I ask You for . . .
or
I give You . . .

End the prayer standing up, with your hands folded over your heart.

Make me a vessel of Your grace—pour Your love and mercy into me. Let Your compassion and goodness flow through me, and water the world with Your beautiful grace.

Amen.

A VESSEL OF GRACE

As you move and pray, turn your attention to the ways God can and is using you as a vessel of His grace to the people around you. Awaken your senses to the evidence of His love and mercy in your own life, and let it flow like a river through you, filling you with His strength and peace, and overflowing with grace that touches everyone you meet.

When we move through our days in a rhythm of prayer, when we're mindful of His love and presence with us at all times in every circumstance, we're able to rest in knowing that no matter what is happening around us, we are safe and held and loved. This allows us to move out into the world with a full heart and a calm mind so that we can experience this beautiful life God has given us and share His love with those around us.

Therefore, brothers and sisters, in view of the mercies of God,
I urge you to present your bodies as a living sacrifice, holy
and pleasing to God; this is your true worship.
ROMANS 12:1 CSB

An example of my own body map, drawn on a day when I was feeling some pain and anxiety, and remembering some of the stories and scars I carry.

BODY MAPPING

Body mapping is a body awareness tool that allows you to visually observe, describe, and draw the story of your body. This activity can help you connect with your body in a positive way, allowing you to increase in compassion and gratitude toward your body.

Make sure you have a sheet of paper, markers, pens, or colored pencils. (Other art supplies are optional—you can get as creative as you'd like with this activity.)

DRAW AN OUTLINE OF THE SHAPE OF YOUR BODY

- You don't have to be an artist; just draw something to represent your body.

TAKE A MOMENT TO TUNE IN TO YOURSELF

- Begin by taking a deep breath in and a full exhale.
- Allow your attention to be drawn to how you are feeling. Ask yourself: *What do I notice in my body? What needs my attention right now? Are there any images, feelings, physical sensations, or points of constriction?*
- Invite God into this space with you. Ask Him to reveal an area that needs care.

INTUITIVELY DRAW THE AREAS THAT ARE RESPONDING

- Draw the areas where you notice that some feeling or emotion is present. Don't overthink this part; just let yourself flow with it.
- You can also consider past stories your body is carrying—scars you wear on your skin or in your soul. Draw these areas on your body as well.
- You can use different colors, shades, or symbols if that is helpful. You can also get more creative and use other materials if you'd like, such as yarn, scraps of fabric, paint, scrapbook paper, or stickers.
- Express the sensations and emotions you notice, with compassion toward yourself and without judgment.
- As you work, you can pray. Tell God your story (nothing surprises Him; He already knows everything about you), and invite Him to pour His mercy, love, and grace over your story.

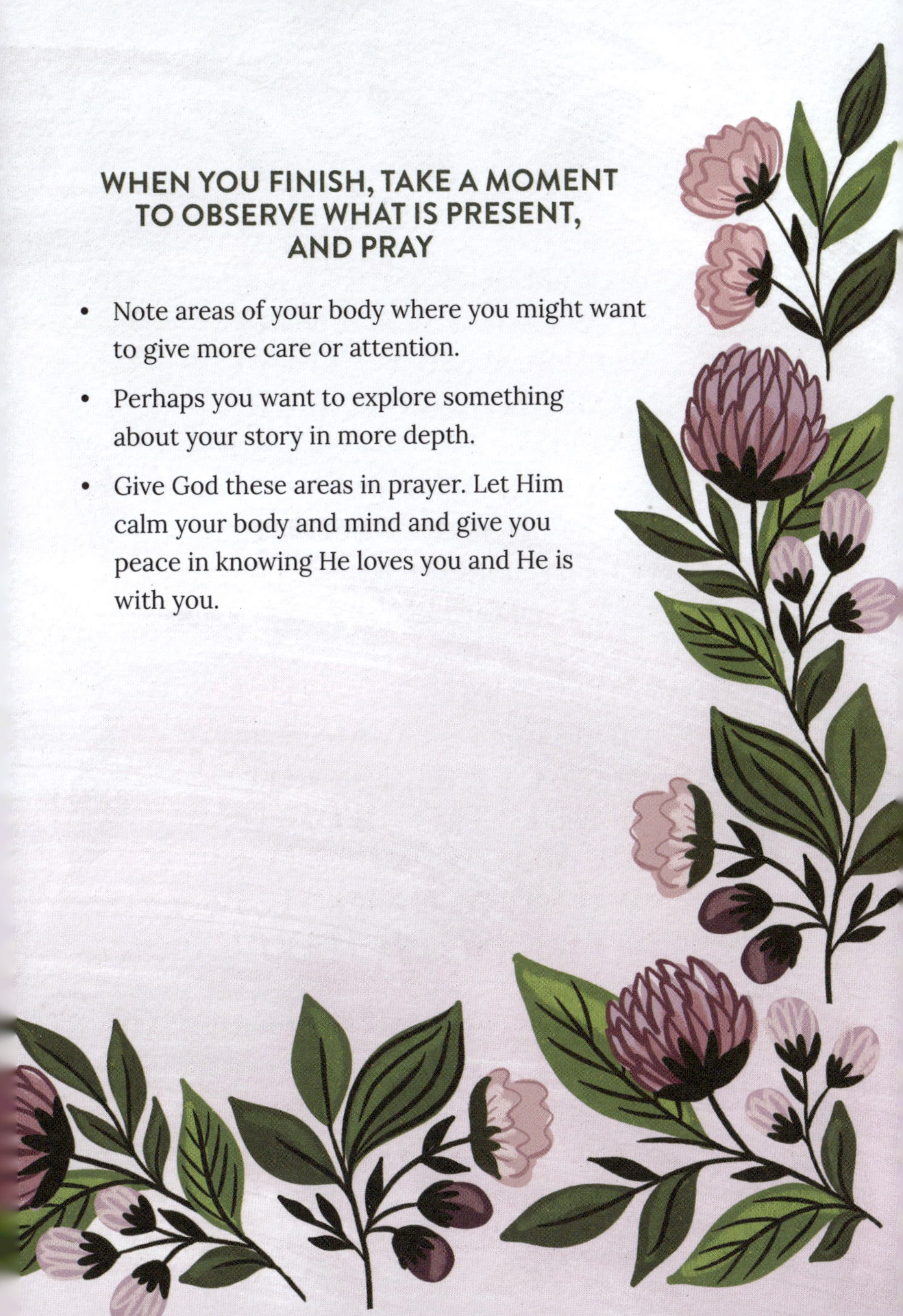

WHEN YOU FINISH, TAKE A MOMENT TO OBSERVE WHAT IS PRESENT, AND PRAY

- Note areas of your body where you might want to give more care or attention.
- Perhaps you want to explore something about your story in more depth.
- Give God these areas in prayer. Let Him calm your body and mind and give you peace in knowing He loves you and He is with you.

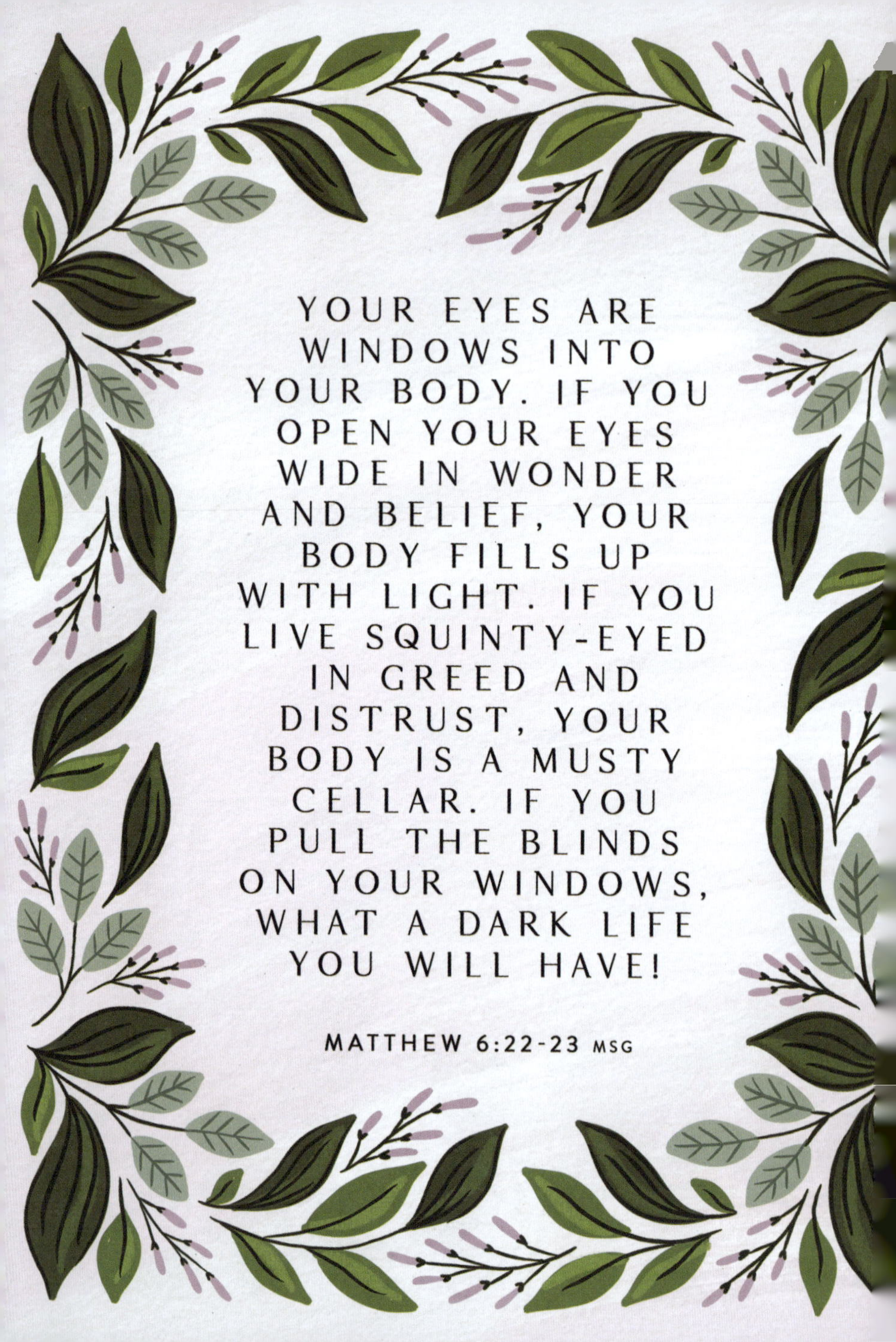
YOUR EYES ARE
WINDOWS INTO
YOUR BODY. IF YOU
OPEN YOUR EYES
WIDE IN WONDER
AND BELIEF, YOUR
BODY FILLS UP
WITH LIGHT. IF YOU
LIVE SQUINTY-EYED
IN GREED AND
DISTRUST, YOUR
BODY IS A MUSTY
CELLAR. IF YOU
PULL THE BLINDS
ON YOUR WINDOWS,
WHAT A DARK LIFE
YOU WILL HAVE!
MATTHEW 6:22-23 MSG

CONNECT WITH NATURE

Connecting with nature—noticing our natural surroundings and appreciating the gift of creation—can greatly support our mental and physical health by reducing stress and promoting healing.[59] Research shows that "people who are more connected with nature are usually happier in life and more likely to report feeling their lives are worthwhile. Nature can generate many positive emotions such as calmness, joy, and creativity and can facilitate concentration."[60] When we spend time outdoors with others, we can create shared experiences that strengthen emotional bonds and foster a sense of belonging.

- Walk barefoot outside.
- Lie on the ground and look up at the sky.
- Collect nature objects to feel.
- Connect with animals.
- Go bird watching and listen to birdsong.
- Smell the flowers.
- Sit near a body of water and listen to the sounds.
- Plant a garden.
- Go for a hike.

EMBODIED PRAYER

Use the movements of the "Butterfly Hug" on page 88 for this prayer:

Cross your arms over your chest as if you're hugging yourself.
Gently tap your upper arms, alternating left and right slowly to the rhythm of the prayer:
"In the places . . .": tap right;
"fill me with . . .": tap left.

All-knowing Father,

In the places I feel pain,
fill me with Your peace.

In the places I feel inadequate,
fill me with Your grace.

In the places I can't move,
fill me with Your love.

In the places I am sick,
fill me with Your mercy.

In the places I feel weak,
fill me with Your strength.

Until the day You make all things new and whole, may my limitations keep me turning and returning to You.

Continue hugging yourself, envisioning God's loving arms holding you.

No matter how my body may fail,
You will never fail me.
You are mine forever.

Amen.

UNTIL THE DAY

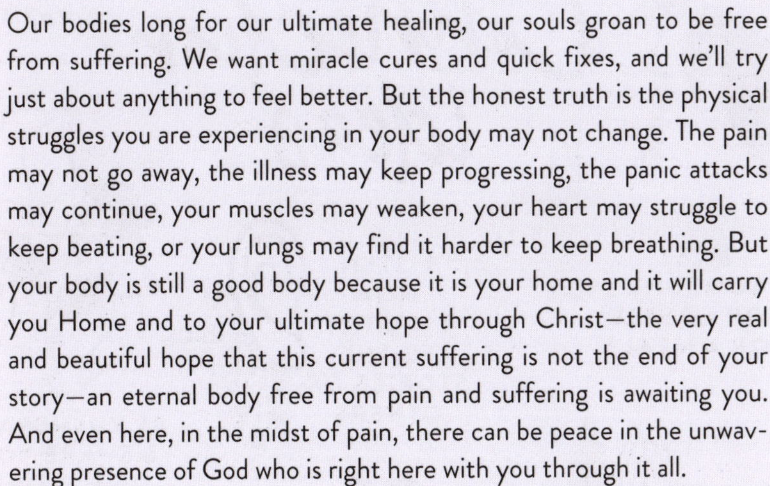

As you move and pray, turn your attention to any pain or discomfort you may be feeling today. Invite God into those places of pain, and accept the hope and peace that only He can give.

Our bodies long for our ultimate healing, our souls groan to be free from suffering. We want miracle cures and quick fixes, and we'll try just about anything to feel better. But the honest truth is the physical struggles you are experiencing in your body may not change. The pain may not go away, the illness may keep progressing, the panic attacks may continue, your muscles may weaken, your heart may struggle to keep beating, or your lungs may find it harder to keep breathing. But your body is still a good body because it is your home and it will carry you Home and to your ultimate hope through Christ—the very real and beautiful hope that this current suffering is not the end of your story—an eternal body free from pain and suffering is awaiting you. And even here, in the midst of pain, there can be peace in the unwavering presence of God who is right here with you through it all.

My health may fail, and my spirit may grow weak, but God remains the strength of my heart; he is mine forever.

PSALM 73:26

More Connection ideas

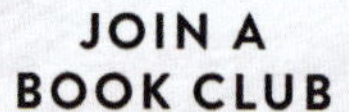

JOIN A BOOK CLUB

CHOOSE IN-PERSON OVER ONLINE WHEN POSSIBLE

CONNECT WITH A THERAPIST

REACH OUT TO A FRIEND

EXPRESS & RECEIVE GRATITUDE

MEET SOMEONE FOR COFFEE OR A MEAL

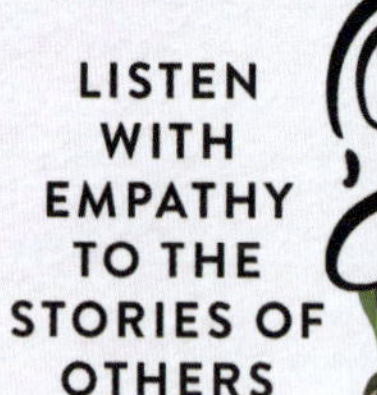

LISTEN WITH EMPATHY TO THE STORIES OF OTHERS

BE VULNERABLE & SHARE YOUR OWN STORIES

PRAY FOR OTHERS

CONTRIBUTE TO SOMETHING LARGER THAN YOURSELF

BE PRESENT

NOTES

1. Adapted from a sermon by Daniel DeForest London, "The Celtic Way of Embodied Prayer: Mary, Maewyn and Meyg," Daniel DeForest London, March 17, 2013, https://deforestlondon.wordpress.com/2013/03/17/the-celtic-way-of-embodied-prayer-mary-maewyn-and-meyg; his name being "Maewyn" is largely debated with no primary sources, so it is likely the result of stories and folklore passed down through the centuries.

2. Sandra Pavloff Conner, *Patrick: Servant of Jesus Christ: The True Story of One of God's Most Amazing Soul Winners: St. Patrick of Ireland* (St. Ellen Press, 2020), Kindle.

3. A Collection of Prayers, https://acollectionofprayers.com/2016/07/01/st-patricks-creed/.

4. Fr. Neil Xavier O'Donoghue, *St. Patrick: His Confession and Other Works* (Catholic Book Publishing Co. 2009), 16.

5. Conner, *Patrick: Servant of Jesus Christ.*

6. Tyler Staton, *Praying Like Monks, Living Like Fools* (Thomas Nelson, 2022), 194.

7. Joan Chittister, *The Monastic Heart* (Convergent Books, 2022), 40.

8. Chittister, Joan. The Monastic Heart: 50 Simple Practices For a Contemplative and Fulfilling Life. p.13

9. "Nervous System," Cleveland Clinic, last reviewed Nov. 16, 2023, https://my.clevelandclinic.org/health/body/21202-nervous-system.

10. Howard E. LeWine, MD, reviewer, "Understanding the Stress Response: Chronic Activation of This Survival Mechanism Impairs Health," Harvard Health, April 3, 2024, https://www.health.harvard.edu/staying-healthy/understanding-the-stress-response.

11. Hillary L. McBride, *The Wisdom of Your Body: Finding Healing, Wholeness, and Connection through Embodied Living* (Brazos Press, 2021), 60–61.

12. "Parasympathetic Nervous System," Cleveland Clinic, last reviewed June 6, 2022, https://my.clevelandclinic.org/health/body/23266-parasympathetic-nervous-system-psns.

13. "Good Stress, Bad Stress," Stanford Medicine, December 21, 2012, https://med.stanford.edu/news/all-news/2012/12/good-stress-bad-stress.html.

14. Britt Piper (@healwithbritt), Instagram, https://www.instagram.com/healwithbritt/.

15. LeWine, "Understanding the Stress Response."

16. McBride, *The Wisdom of Your Body*, 56–57.

17. Substance Abuse and Mental Health Services Administration. "Understanding the Impact of Trauma" in *Trauma-Informed Care in Behavioral Health Services. Treatment Improvement Protocol (TIP) Series 57*. (Substance Abuse and Mental Health Services Administration, 2014), https://www.ncbi.nlm.nih.gov/books/NBK207191/./

18. Kelly McGonigal, *The Joy of Movement* (Penguin Publishing Group, 2021), 191–193, Kindle.

19. McGonigal, *The Joy of Movement*, 191.

20. McGonigal, *The Joy of Movement*, 191.

21. "Somatic Self Care," Johns Hopkins Medicine, https://www.hopkinsmedicine.org/office-of-well-being/connection-support/somatic-self-care.

22. Bessel van der Kolk, *The Body Keeps the Score: Brain, Mind, and Body in the Healing of Trauma* (Penguin Books, 2021), 64.

23 Daniela Ramirez-Duran, "Somatic Experiencing Therapy: 10 Best Exercises & Examples," PositivePsychology.com, November 11, 2020, https://positivepsychology.com/somatic-experiencing/.

24. Leslie Riopel, "PANAS Scale: The Positive and Negative Affect Schedule," PositivePsychology.com, August 20, 2019, https://positivepsychology.com/positive-and-negative-affect-schedule-panas/.

25. Amy G. Oden, *Right Here Right Now: The Practice of Christian Mindfulness* (Abingdon Press, 2017), 51.

26. Adapted from Christopher Willard, "A Quick, Calming Body Scan to Check in With Yourself," *Mindful*, April 3, 2020, https://www.mindful.org/a-quick-calming-body-scan-to-check-in-with-yourself/.

27. Emily P. Freeman (@emilypfreeman), Instagram, March 18, 2025, https://www.instagram.com/p/DHVplCcvjMZ.

28. Natalie Gale, "How Glimmers Can Alleviate Our Triggers," The Good Trade, October 30, 2023, https://www.thegoodtrade.com/features/glimmers-and-triggers/.

29. Melis Yilmaz Balban, et al., "Brief Structured Respiration Practices Enhance Mood and Reduce Physiological Arousal." *Cell Reports. Medicine* vol 4, no. 1 (2023): 100895, https://pmc.ncbi.nlm.nih.gov/articles/PMC9873947/.

30. Sesame Workshop, "Butterfly Breathing with Abby Cadabby," https://sesameworkshop.org/resources/butterfly-breathing-with-abby-cadabby/.

31. Hadley Leggett, "'Cyclic sighing' Can Help Breathe Away Anxiety," Stanford Medicine, February 9, 2023, https://scopeblog.stanford.edu/2023/02/09/cyclic-sighing-can-help-breathe-away-anxiety/.

32. "Transforming Lives through Healing Trauma," Somatic Experiencing International, https://traumahealing.org/.

33. Crystal Raypole, "Yes, You Can (and Should) Give Yourself a Hug," Healthline, June 17, 2020, https://www.healthline.com/health/hugging-self.

34. "Health Benefits of Gratitude," UCLA Health, March 22, 2023, https://www.uclahealth.org/news/article/health-benefits-gratitude.

35. Kirsten Weir, "Nurtured by Nature," American Psychological Association, April 8, 2025, https://www.apa.org/monitor/2020/04/nurtured-nature.

36. Marcia P. Jimenez, et al., "Associations between Nature Exposure and Health: A Review of the Evidence," National Library of Medicine, PubMed Central, April 30, 2021, https://pmc.ncbi.nlm.nih.gov/articles/PMC8125471/.

37. Frontiers, "Stressed? Take a 20-minute 'Nature Pill,'" ScienceDaily, April 4, 2019, https://www.sciencedaily.com/releases/2019/04/190404074915.htm.

38. Qing Li, "'Forest Bathing' Is Great for Your Health. Here's How to Do It," *TIME*, May 1, 2018, https://time.com/5259602/japanese-forest-bathing/.

39. Ann Voskamp, "A Spa for Your Soul: 5 Proven Secrets to Rest & Revive (Instead of Being Overwhelmed and Exhausted)," Annvoskamp.com, https://annvoskamp.com/2023/05/a-spa-for-your-soul-5-proven-secrets-to-rest-revive-instead-of-being-overwhelmed-exhausted/.

40. Mark Buchanan, *God Walk: Moving at the Speed of Your Soul* (Zondervan, 2020), 115–116.

41. Buchanan, *God Walk*, 115–116.

42. Adapted from Irene Kraegel, *A Mindful Moment: 5-Minute Meditations and Devotions* (ZonderKidz 2022), 168–169.

43. Alyssa Hunt, "The Power of Walking: Steps to Better Health," Loma Linda University Health, June 20, 2024, https://news.llu.edu/health-wellness/power-of-walking-steps-better-health.

44. Gordon Gooding, "What is Bilateral Stimulation and How Can It Help?" Gooding Wellness Group, updated July 23, 2024, https://www.goodingwellness.com/post/what-is-bilateral-stimulation.

45 Adapted from Jason Hobbs and Dena Hobbs, *When Anxiety Strikes: Help and Hope for Managing Your Storm* (Kregel Publications, 2020), 137–138.

46. Adapted from Christine Byrne, "What Is Somatic Stretching? How It Works, Benefits, and Stretches for Beginners," Everyday Health, May 22, 2024, https://www.everydayhealth.com/fitness/what-is-somatic-stretching/.

47. Adapted from Byrne, "What Is Somatic Stretching?"

48. Adapted from Byrne, "What Is Somatic Stretching.?"

49. Adapted from Hobbs, *When Anxiety Strikes*, 56–57.

50. McBride, *The Wisdom of Your Body*, 65.

51. Christopher Bergland, "How Self-Initiated Laughter Can Make You Feel Better," Psychology Today, September 18, 2016, https://www.psychologytoday.com/us/blog/the-athletes-way/201609/how-self-initiated-laughter-can-make-you-feel-better.

52. Elena Davydova, "The Transformative Power of Creative Arts: Nurturing Mental Health Through Expression," GPS Possibility Partners, July 19, 2023, https://www.guidetopersonalsolutions.com/post/the-transformative-power-of-creative-arts-nurturing-mental-health-through-expression.

53. Dr. Chris Mosunic, reviewer, "What Is Co-regulation in Relationships?" Calm, May 7, https://www.calm.com/blog/co-regulation.

54. Mosunic, "What is co-regulation in relationships?"

55 Sara Berg, "What Doctors Wish Patients Knew About Loneliness and Health," AMA, July 14, 2023, https://www.ama-assn.org/public-health/behavioral-health/what-doctors-wish-patients-knew-about-loneliness-and-health.

56 Kelli Harding, "How Loneliness Impacts Your Health—and Ways to Make Connections," Columbia Doctors, July 11, 2024, https://www.columbiadoctors.org/news/how-loneliness-impacts-your-health-and-ways-make-connections.

57 "Alone but Not Lonely: How Solitude Boosts Wellbeing," University of Reading, December 5, 2023, https://www.reading.ac.uk/news/2023/Research-News/How-solitude-boosts-wellbeing.

58. "Health Effects of Social Isolation and Loneliness," CDC Social Connection, May 15, 2024, https://www.cdc.gov/social-connectedness/risk-factors/index.html.

59. Jim Robbins, "Ecopsychology: How Immersion in Nature Benefits Your Health," Yale Environment 360, January 9, 2020, https://e360.yale.edu/features/ecopsychology-how-immersion-in-nature-benefits-your-health.

60. "Nature: How Connecting with Nature Benefits Our Mental Health," Mental Health Foundation, https://www.mentalhealth.org.uk/our-work/research/nature-how-connecting-nature-benefits-our-mental-health.

Embrace a daily practice of abiding with Christ.

Find hope amid anxiety through the spiritual practice of breath prayer in this beautifully illustrated and practical guide to connecting body, mind, and spirit during times of stress.

Breath as Prayer will lead you through the practice and the proven health benefits of Christian breath prayer: intentional prayers centered around Scripture that focus our minds on Christ as we calm our bodies through breathing.

***Breath as Prayer* offers:**

- More than 80 breath prayers focused on Scripture, along with brief meditations
- Gorgeous original full-color illustrations
- A quick-start how-to guide to refer to as needed
- Guidance on how to implement a breath prayer practice
- The science behind breath work and prayer and why it works
- An invitation to reflect on the effect of breath prayers on your body

Breathe deeply, lean into God's Word, and discover why every breath can be an invitation to pray.

Breath prayers can be done
at any time and anywhere
you are able to slow down,
be still, and breathe.

BREATHING TECHNIQUES

365

three times per day, six breaths per minute, five-minute duration

- Inhale slowly through the nose for **five** seconds
- Exhale slowly through the mouth for **five** seconds
- Repeat for **five** minutes

4-7-8 (THE RELAXING BREATH)

- Inhale slowly through the nose for a count of **four**
- Hold your breath for a count of **seven**
- Exhale completely through your mouth for a count of **eight**
- Repeat the cycle three more times for a total of four breaths

SQUARE BREATHING

(also called "box breathing")

- Inhale slowly through the nose for a count of **four**
- Hold your breath for a count of **four**
- Exhale slowly through the mouth for a count of **four**
- Hold your breath for a count of **four**

GOD IS YOUR SHEPHERD

Breathe Deep and Know: *The good Shepherd is with you. You have everything you need.*

One of the most beautiful and comforting pictures of how God loves and cares for us is when He is shown as a shepherd caring for His sheep. Jesus Himself tells us, "I am the good shepherd; I know my own sheep, and they know me" (John 10:14).

A flock of sheep is fully dependent on their shepherd. On their own, domesticated sheep are prone to wander, exposed to danger, unable to right themselves if they fall and they can even have trouble finding their own food or water. But under the care and guidance of a loving shepherd, sheep are led safely to bountiful green pastures, protected from dangerous predators, picked up and steadied when they fall, and guided back to the flock when they are spooked or start to wander away. Sheep can actually recognize their shepherd's face and they know their shepherd's voice. They trust their shepherd and depend on him to provide everything they need.

As your good shepherd, the Lord is lovingly guiding you and providing for you today. No matter your circumstances or the path that this life has you on, the Lord, your shepherd, is with you. You don't have to worry or be afraid. Simply stay with the Shepherd. With Him, you will always have all that you need.

The Lord is my shepherd; I have all that I need.

PSALM 23:1

inhale:

THE LORD IS MY SHEPHERD,

exhale:

I HAVE ALL THAT I NEED.

INHALE:

I give my burdens to You;

EXHALE:

You will take care of me.

Still your soul and rest your mind.

Do you notice that even when your body is not moving, your mind is racing? Anxiety, to-do lists, and the spiral of negative thought patterns often keep us from the stillness we long for. In *Present in Prayer*, award-winning author Jennifer Tucker invites you to allow the Holy Spirit to speak through God's Word and renew your mind through the practice of Christian meditation.

As in her first book, *Breath as Prayer*, Jennifer shares a powerful prayer practice in this beautifully illustrated book that is deep yet accessible. Each of the 30 meditations offers you:

- A gentle call to silence, an opening prayer, and a thoughtful reflection on a Bible verse
- Guided meditation on Scripture using the centuries-old practice of *lectio divina*—a framework of Christian meditation that helps you slow down and linger on God's Word
- A prayer of surrender and prompts for how to live out the truths God is speaking to you
- Inspired art to draw you into each meditation as you consider what is lovely, true, excellent, and worthy of praise

You're not in a hurry. You're on a journey. Cultivate a more purposeful and peaceful prayer life and greater intimacy with God as you focus your thoughts on His Word.

1

THE WORD OF GOD IS TRUE

PSALM 119:159–168

If we're going to fix our minds on whatever is true, then God Himself and His Word should be our first focus. God's Word is the source of truth because God Himself is true.

David knew this. Over and over throughout the book of Psalms, we see him and other psalmists turn to God and His Word. Psalm 33:4 declares, "For the word of the Lord holds true, and we can trust everything he does," and Psalm 19:7 says, "The instructions of the Lord are perfect, reviving the soul." Psalm 119 in particular is filled with continual expressions of love for the instructions, laws, and promises of God. In fact, God's written revelation, His Word, is referred to in at least 171 of the 176 verses.

In verses 159–168 David expressed his love for God's Word—a love rooted in the firm belief that God can be trusted and everything He says is true. David also expressed his hatred for falsehood and lies, because lying is in opposition to truth and God's Word and doesn't produce anything good, but the love of truth—the love of God's instruction, of His Word—brings "abundant peace" (v. 165 HCSB).

Silence

Begin with a time of silence.

Still your body. . . . Slow your breathing. . . . Quiet your mind.

Focus on being fully present in this moment,
right here, right now.

the entirety of your word is truth.

PSALM 119:160 CSB

Consider how I love your precepts; LORD, give me life according to your faithful love. The entirety of your word is truth, each of your righteous judgments endures forever. Princes have persecuted me without cause, but my heart fears only your word. I rejoice over your promise like one who finds vast treasure. I hate and abhor falsehood, but I love your instruction. I praise you seven times a day for your righteous judgments. Abundant peace belongs to those who love your instruction; nothing makes them stumble. LORD, I hope for your salvation and carry out your commands. I obey your decrees and love them greatly. I obey your precepts and decrees, for all my ways are before you.

PSALM 119:159–168 CSB

Opening Prayer

God of all truth,

I bring my whole self to You right now—
just as I am.
Help me to focus my mind on You today.
Turn my thoughts to the truth
of Your Word.

I invite You to speak to me,
to search my heart and shape my life.
Show me what is true.

Open my eyes to see You.
Open my ears to hear Your voice.
Open my heart to receive Your Word.
Open my hands to accept whatever
You give.

Draw close to me, Lord,
as I draw close to You.

Amen.

Read & Meditate

Read through the Bible passage three times, taking time to pause and pray and quietly listen to the Holy Spirit speaking to your heart.

LECTIO 1: READ THROUGH THE PASSAGE SLOWLY.

What is one word or phrase that stands out to you?

....

PAUSE & PRAY

In silence, meditate on this word or phrase.

LECTIO 2: READ THROUGH THE PASSAGE A SECOND TIME.

This time, pray through the passage, reading phrase by phrase. Talk to God, pausing to listen and respond to Him as you read.

PAUSE & PRAY

In silence, bring your attention to the present moment.

LECTIO 3: READ THROUGH THE PASSAGE A THIRD TIME.

Sit in stillness again as you contemplate the word or phrase that stood out to you and how it may apply to your life right now.

NOTICE

Notice your body: What are you feeling right now?
Notice your thoughts: What are you thinking right now?
Notice your circumstances: What is happening in your life right now?

Compassionately consider these things, and listen to what the Holy Spirit may be revealing to you in light of today's reading and meditation. What invitation might God be extending to you today?

God is inviting me to . . .

....

....

....

Surrendering Prayer

As I prepare to enter into the rest of my day, Lord,

Calm the lies in my head
and the fears that steal my peace.
Help me to turn my mind to truth
and to trust Your loving heart for me.

May my pace be slow and unhurried,
ever aware of Your presence with me.

May my mind be attentive and clear,
noticing the gift of every moment.

May my heart be gentle and kind,
showing compassion to myself and others.

Today, I give You my worries,
and I choose to trust the truth of Your Word.

Keep turning my thoughts to whatever is true.
Transform me to be more like You.

Amen.

Embody

Continue to contemplate the word and invitation God gave you today.

Consider: What are some lies that your fears are telling you today? What truth can you intentionally focus on instead?

ABOUT THE AUTHOR

Jennifer Tucker is an illustrator, lettering artist, and bestselling author. Her artwork has been featured in multiple publications and books, including *The Message Canvas Bible* and the ECPA bestselling coloring book *Whatever Is Lovely*, and she received the 2023 ECPA Christian Book Award for New Author of the Year for her first book, *Breath as Prayer: Calm Your Anxiety, Focus Your Mind, and Renew your Soul*. Jennifer is a devoted follower of Jesus and an advocate for mental health. She lives in Georgia with her family, and she shares her heart and art online at littlehousestudio.net. Connect with Jennifer on Instagram @jenn_littlehousestudio.

Also by the Author

Breath As Prayer: *Calm Your Anxiety, Focus Your Mind, and Renew Your Soul*

Present in Prayer: *A Guided Invitation to Peace Through Biblical Meditation*